*A*mericans are increasingly concerned about saving for retirement, and with good reason. People are living longer and retiring earlier. Traditional pensions are declining and Washington is filled with talk of changing Social Security.

There are a number of resources available that can help you learn about saving for retirement. What we believed was missing was reliable, easy-to-understand information about what to do with your savings when you are ready to retire, and the valuable role annuities can play in helping you achieve your retirement goals.

In addition to laying out the choices you'll have in creating your own retirement income, this book answers such questions as:

- Which savings plans are designed to provide retirement income, and which are better suited to leaving an estate to heirs?

- What am I responsible for when I begin to receive income from my retirement savings? What regulations should I be aware of, and what steps do I have to take to get what I want, when I want it?

- How will my retirement income be taxed, and are there ways to reduce the amount of tax I'll pay on this income?

- Why should I consider an annuity, and how does an annuity differ from my other options?

Choices you make in your retirement savings strategy, whether before or after you retire, will have an impact on the quality of life you can enjoy as a retired person.

With careful planning and the right information, retirement can be one of the most rewarding times of your life. We hope this book can serve as a helpful resource to make your own personal vision a reality.

Mark J. Mackey
President & CEO
NAVA

CREATING RETIREMENT INCOME

CREATING RETIREMENT INCOME

VIRGINIA B. MORRIS

LIGHTBULB PRESS

LIGHTBULB PRESS
Project Team
Design Director Dave Wilder
Editorial Karen W. Lichtenberg, Karen Halloran Meldrom
Production Holly Duthie, Kara Hatch, Thomas F. Trojan
Illustration Krista K. Glasser
Contributors Roy Higgins, John Fried, Craig Lauer

SPECIAL THANKS
Special thanks to the following companies for their support of this book
Conseco, Equitable—Member of the Global AXA Group, Fidelity Investments Life Insurance Company, Keyport Life Insurance Company, Lincoln National Life Insurance Company, MetLife, New York Life, SunAmerica, Inc., SunLife of Canada, Templeton Funds Annuity Company, The Variable Annuity Life Insurance Company (VALIC), USAA Life Insurance Company.

Special thanks to the NAVA Editorial Committee
for their wisdom and expertise

Special thanks to members of the NAVA staff
for their contributions to this book

PICTURE CREDITS
Stephen Derr/The Image Bank, New York (page 50)

LIGHTBULB PRESS

CONTENTS

Retirement—You're at the Helm

Finding a secure retirement means charting the right course.

People who are living comfortable retirements today typically count on income from traditional pensions, Social Security, their investments, and sometimes profits from selling their homes to anchor their financial security. But what lies ahead when you look forward to your own retirement?

Current retirement lifestyles are likely to be hard to match unless you're able to provide a major share of the income you'll need from your own investments. That's because two of the traditional mainstays—employer-sponsored pensions and Social Security—will probably provide less of what you'll need than they did for your parents.

IT'S NOT PANIC TIME

Building an investment portfolio over time may be the best approach to producing the retirement income you need, but it's not the only way. If you get lump sum payouts or bonuses from your employer, inherit money, or even win the lottery, you can use the money to make smart investments

THE CHALLENGE

If you don't have a pension, haven't contributed as much as you can to a retirement saving plan, and aren't investing on your own, the prospect of being responsible for producing retirement income may seem overwhelming. But it's also a wake-up call.

That's true in part because reverting to the older pattern of living with your children and grandchildren in retirement is unlikely—even if it sounds appealing—since family structures have changed dramatically. Women who were the traditional caregivers are increasingly working outside the home. And retirement periods can last 20 or 30 years, or even longer, a long time to share living space.

RETIREMENT RESOURCES

The good old days

The new reality

If you've wondered why providing retirement income is a major topic of discussion, consider these numbers. According to the Census Bureau, there were 3 million people over 65 in the U.S. in 1900, about 4% of the population. By 2050, that number will be 82 million, or 20% of the population.

to help guarantee a comfortable retirement. The more you know about how various investments work, the kinds of income they can provide, and the ways you can make them grow, the smarter the financial decisions you can make.

THE SANDWICH GENERATION

Tomorrow's retirement generation may have to cope with an added complication.

Managing on your retirement income can be tougher if you still have children living at home or are helping them pay college tuition, buy a home or get established in their own business. If, in addition, your parents depend on you for support or you're helping to cover their health care costs, you may find you can't afford to live as you'd like.

If it's any consolation, many people are finding themselves financially sandwiched in supporting younger and older generations. The Census Bureau reports that between 43% and 56% of 18 to 24 year-olds live with their parents. And the Agency for Healthcare Research and Quality says that 29% of adult children have some financial responsibility for a retired parent.

What this boils down to is needing extra income in your early retirement years if your parents or children need your financial support.

DOING YOUR PART

The income that can make the difference between having the money you need in retirement or being pinched for cash comes from long-term investments you make during your working life and investment decisions you continue to make after you retire.

What you're aiming for is income you can count on, year in and year out, to supplement the checks you get from Social Security and any pension you might expect.

There are other reasons to invest, of course. Investments help you pay for other things that are important to you, such as your own home or your children's education. Investments also let you build an estate to leave to your heirs. And for many people, investing is just plain fun, a way to test their ability to make smart choices.

But none of these is more important than the investment decisions you make to provide sufficient income that will last for as long as you live.

Living Longer

An increasing number of people will spend as much time in retirement as they did working.

Longer retirements aren't a sign that people don't like to work. Rather, they reflect the increasingly long lives that people are living. It's not unusual to follow a 35-year career with an equally long retirement. In fact, today your retirement will typically last almost twice as long as your childhood, and the way you live will continue to change, just as it did as you grew up.

By 2050, experts predict there'll be one million people over 100 years old, a notable increase from the 40,000 centarians alive in 1998. This longevity is even more striking when compared to the normal life expectancy at the turn of the last century—which was just 49.

IT'S NOT JUST A PHASE

Retirement, like childhood, is a catch-all term that describes several distinct phases in your life.

If you retire at 55 to start a second career or spend more time doing the things you love, your retirement experience is very different from someone who is also retired but age 85—your parents, for example, or a former teacher or employer.

One of the most important differences between early and late retirement is how you spend your money—and sometimes the amount you need to live comfortably. Medical expenses may increase as you get older, for example, while some other costs are likely to shrink or even disappear.

But as long as you're retired, you need a steady source of income. It won't surprise you to learn that many people's greatest fear is outliving their resources—a situation they describe as living too long.

EARLY RETIREMENT	LATER RETIREMENT
Active hobbies	Fewer activities
Travel	Less travel
Support for children or aging parents	Independent children and no parental care
Good health	Declining health

THE RULE OF 72

A little quick math, using a formula called the rule of 72, demonstrates the impact of inflation and emphasizes why you need more income every year you're retired to maintain your lifestyle. Just divide the number 72 by the inflation rate to estimate how quickly the prices you're paying now will double.

At an average rate of 3.1%, for example, a basket of groceries that cost you $60 in 2002 would be up to $120 by 2025 (72 ÷ 3.1 = 23.22 years). And if inflation were higher, as it was in the 1980s, prices would increase even more quickly.

THE SHRINKING DOLLAR
One easy way to see the impact of inflation is to track food prices. Look what has happened to the cost of a loaf of white bread.

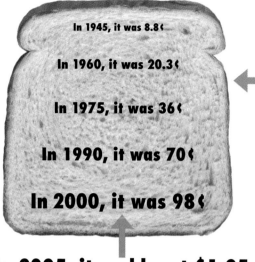

In 1945, it was 8.8¢

In 1960, it was 20.3¢

In 1975, it was 36¢

In 1990, it was 70¢

In 2000, it was 98¢

By 2005, it could cost $1.25

For example
1960   2001

Cup of coffee
$.10 $1.00

Quart of milk
$.27 $.99

Burger, fries and cola
$.49 $4.98

Gallon of gas
$.30 $1.72

Movie ticket
$1.00 $8.50

THE INFLATION FACTOR
Inflation is one reason it's smart to be concerned about outliving your assets—even if you expect to spend less as you get older. The easiest explanation of how inflation works is that as time passes, prices tend to go up. Another way to put it is that over time money gradually loses its buying power.

Whatever your age, you can remember when you paid less for something and often got more—whether you're thinking of a chocolate bar, a double feature at the movies or your first car. And there are noticeably fewer things—some electronic products may be an exception—that cost less than they once did.

While there are times when inflation is low—a rate of increase around 3% a year has been the historical average in the U.S. since 1925—there are also times when inflation gallops along, pulling prices with it. Experts caution that even relatively low inflation erodes your buying power if you have a **fixed income**, which stays constant from year to year.

WHY INFLATION HAPPENS
The classic explanation for inflation has been that it increases more quickly in periods of prosperity, and slows down during recessions, when demand for products and services drops off. What no one can ever predict is the pace of an economic cycle.

The pattern was different in the 1990s, a period of growth and low inflation. Experts haven't agreed on an explanation for this change. And, they add, it would be foolish to assume that periods of greater inflation are a thing of the past.

THE FINANCIAL FACTS OF LIFE
The older you get, the more difficulty you're likely to have supplementing a fixed income with second jobs or loans. Fair or not, lenders want to be sure you'll have enough money to keep up your payments, something they often equate with a steady job. Your chances of finding good-paying jobs, part- or full-time, decrease with age, too. And your willingness to work, or your ability to handle the hours, might diminish as well.

Those factors contribute to the sense of urgency many people feel about accumulating enough investment resources so that they'll have access to the income they need. Surveys show that what older adults worry about most is outliving their resources and having to become dependent on family members.

The projected percentages of U.S. residents 65 and older:

Year	Percentage
2010	13.2%
2020	16.5%
2030	20%
2050	20.3%

Source:
US Bureau of the Census

Early Retirement

Retirements aren't only lasting longer.
They're starting earlier.

When you think retirement, you may think 65. Since the 1930s, when Social Security was introduced and employee pensions became increasingly common, that's been the traditional retirement age. At 65, you're eligible for Medicare, which was designed to provide health care coverage for retired people. And 65 is when you get a small break on your taxes by being eligible to take an additional personal exemption.

Despite the pull of tradition, and the financial advantages that sometimes go with retiring at 65, most people are not waiting that long. The average retirement age by 1998 was down to 63.

Earlier?

50 years

- **Less time in pension plan**
- **Less in personal investments**
- **Smaller Social Security benefits**
- **Smaller pension payout**

THE EFFECT, IN $s AND ¢s

Financially speaking, the biggest effect of retiring early is having less income. The most obvious reason is that you're not working. But retiring early can also mean a reduction in the retirement income on which you were planning.

To begin with, you'll accumulate fewer years of contributions to your retirement plan. Since you typically earn the highest salary at the end of your career, retiring early means losing contributions based on those amounts. The consequence is usually a smaller pension check than you might have received had you stayed longer.

If all or part of your pension comes from a traditional plan, the amount may also be reduced to offset the greater number of years you are expected to collect—though that policy isn't the same with every employer. Sometimes a pension is based on your salary and the number of years you've worked rather than your age when you retire. In other cases, you can retire with full benefits at age 55.

If you apply for Social Security at 62, the first year you're eligible, you'll receive a smaller amount each year than if you begin collecting at full retirement age of 65 or older. At 62, for example, you get only 80% of what you would have been eligible for had you started benefits at age 65. (People born in 1938 and later will be eligible for an even smaller percentage at age 62 because the age at which full benefits are paid will gradually increase from 65 to 67.)

RETIRED BUT WORKING

People who retire before age 65 tend to continue to work in increasing numbers. One reason seems to be that while you can get your pension and Social Security early, you aren't eligible for Medicare until you reach 65. Plus many employers have been reducing healthcare coverage for retired workers, prompting the need to earn additional income to cover insurance costs.

NEEDING IT LONGER

The other side of retiring early is being retired longer. That means you'll need retirement income for more years. To take a simple example, if you retire at age 60 instead of 65, and need an income of $40,000 a year to live comfortably, you'll increase the amount you need in retirement income resources by $200,000 even before accounting for the impact of inflation.

Income you need	$ 40,000
Years earlier you retire	x 5
Add to resources	= $200,000

What's more, retiring early often means you start withdrawing money from your retirement accounts sooner, reducing the base on which they can grow. That means you need a larger nest egg if you want to ensure your income will last as long as you need it.

WE'LL MISS YOU

65?   Later?

0 years   **70 years**

The traditional retirement age
- Eligible for Medicare
- Eligible for a tax break

- Get the most from your company pension plan
- Get the maximum possible Social Security benefit
- Have more personal investments

THE INVESTMENT DIFFERENCE

Choosing to retire early can also have an impact on your investments. You'll have to stop adding assets to some of them when you're no longer earning a salary. You may have less money to invest in the ones that don't have contribution restrictions. And if you start drawing retirement income from your accounts, they will have less time to grow undisturbed.

The solution is to continue to build the growth component of your portfolio. You can reinvest your earnings in stocks and mutual funds or contribute to a variable annuity. And, if it's financially possible, you can postpone withdrawals from tax-deferred plans. With a traditional IRA, for example, you can wait until you are 70½, and with others even longer.

CALLING IT QUITS

While one of the attractions of early retirement is more time to do the things you enjoy—and maybe less time at a job you've grown tired of—there are other reasons for retiring early.

One is being downsized. While age discrimination is illegal, it's alive and well according to many experts. Older and more highly paid employees may have little choice about early retirement. In that case, having additional sources of long-term income may be crucial.

Or you may be offered an incentive to retire early. Here, you can weigh the benefits of the package that's offered.

WEIGHING THE CHOICE

If you're offered a choice of early retirement packages, here are some questions to ask:

- Will the base on which my traditional pension is figured be increased? By how much?
- Will the offer increase the percentage of my salary that's being replaced?
- If I take a lump sum, is that on top of my regular pension or instead of it?

The advantage of a lump sum payment is that you can invest it to produce another long-term source of income, though a larger pension might add up to more.

Time for Yourself

The promise of retirement is finally having time for what you want to do.

By retiring earlier and living longer, you're likely to have years to do what you like—or to develop new, sometimes unexpected interests. Admittedly, some people find the prospect of retirement disturbing because they're afraid they'll find themselves at loose ends. And there are others who look forward to doing nothing at all. But if you're in the market for new opportunities, you can find them.

NEW CAREERS

When you're eligible to retire, you may decide there is plenty of time to create a second career, either by putting the skills you have to new use or by learning new ones. Figures from the U.S. Bureau of the Census show that about 50% of the people younger than age 62 who are collecting pensions continue to work, as do 25% of those between ages 62 and 65.

That number includes retired executives, who do consulting either for their former employers, for related businesses, or with groups that provide advice to new business owners or nonprofit organizations. It also includes people who work for themselves. AARP, formerly the American Association of Retired Persons, reports that about 230,000 of their members have started new businesses after joining the organization.

NEW ENTHUSIASMS

The best thing about retirement, for most people, is having the time they've craved to spend on things they love to do. You can finally give your hobby the attention it deserves, take the trip you've been postponing or explore activities you haven't had time to try. After all, you control your own time.

Traveling is by far the most popular post-retirement activity. And people whose time is their own can travel in leisurely ways. For example, people over 50 take more than 70% of all the RV trips every year.

The catch is that most activities cost more money than staying put, even after the substantial discounts that retired people qualify for.

Thanks to direct deposits and ATM machines, you don't have to wait for your retirement income checks to arrive before setting off on an adventure. For example, almost 75% of all Social Security payments go directly into bank accounts. Increasingly that's true of pension checks and annuity income payments.

IT'S A DEAL

One of the unexpected advantages of being old enough to retire is that you'll qualify for discounts—sometimes substantial ones—both in the U.S. and abroad. Usually all you have to do is ask.

Most hotel chains will knock at least 10% and sometimes 30% to 50% off the regular rate. You can get good deals on cruises, train tickets, and even airfares, especially if your travel plans are flexible. In fact, the older you are, the more discounts you are eligible for.

Check out publications like The Mature Traveller, Senior Travel Tips and Consumer Reports Travel Letter as well as information from AARP and other affiliations you have, such as alumni organizations and frequent flier clubs.

If you do a little research, you'll find there are a lot of exciting travel opportunities designed for retired people, from Alaskan cruises to scientific research projects.

NEW COMMUNITIES

It may come as no surprise that most people stay put after they retire. Of the 75% of people over 65 who own their own homes—about 10% more than the national average—86% say they plan to continue to live there, according to an AARP survey. And only about 5% move out of state, despite what seems to be a regular exodus to warmer climates.

However, the 1997 tax law revision, which makes up to $500,000 in capital gains on the sale of a married couple's home tax-exempt, may change that. Some experts believe there will be a greater tendency for older adults to move to retirement communities with active educational, athletic, and social schedules.

NEW COMMITMENTS

For many people, retirement is the time to make new commitments to people and organizations that are important to them politically, culturally or emotionally. Volunteer organizations depend on the talents and enthusiasms of these experienced and dedicated workers.

If you're looking for a good cause that needs your help, you can contact The Corporation for National Service at 202-606-5000 or www.nationalservice.org or AARP's The Volunteer Experience at 800-424-3410 or www.aarp.org/volunteerguide.

HELPING OTHERS

In 2001, 7% of those serving in the Peace Corps were older than 50, and about 11,500 served as volunteers in the Service Corps of Retired Executives. Overall, about 44% of all people 55 and older volunteer at least once a year.

Financial Independence

When you have time and money, you can celebrate independence every day.

One big change retirement makes is finally having enough free time to do what you want rather than what you must.

For many people, the most important difference retirement makes is that they have a sense of control over how they spend their time. If they can feel equally confident that they have control over their finances, the stage is set for a rewarding retirement. But while taking control of your life may not require prior planning, taking control of your finances does.

Freedom From Work

If you add up the hours you spend on the job, typically 80,000 over 40 years, or almost 25% of your time, there's little question that retirement can be liberating.

You probably won't have much trouble filling up the time, either with the things you've been postponing or with new interests. In early retirement in particular, you may find you're putting more mileage on the car, spending more time with family and friends, and just generally enjoying yourself.

HEALTHY DECISIONS

While it's not exclusively a financial decision, good healthcare coverage takes a huge burden off your mind. Check the status of your employee health insurance benefits to see if they'll continue, and for how long. If not, investigate the policies available through other groups you belong to, such as professional associations, unions or organizations like AARP, formerly the American Association of Retired Persons. Group coverage is almost always cheaper than individual policies, including insurance you may be eligible for from the company that covered you as an employee.

Medicare solves some of these problems, but you must be 65 to qualify. Since Medicare provides no family coverage, however, you'll still need a plan for your spouse if he or she isn't old enough to qualify.

And be careful. Never drop an insurance policy until you're positive you have a new policy in place.

DOING THE MATH

The tried and true way of figuring out the cost of living in retirement is to list all your current expenses and then estimate what they'll be when you plan to retire and on into your retirement years.

You can do this using a mathematical formula that accounts for:

- The number of years until you plan to retire
- The amount you have already saved
- The anticipated inflation rate
- The estimated real rate of return, or what you earn on your investments after adjusting for inflation

You can find work charts like the one illustrated here to help guide you through the calculation. Often they're in an easy-to-use electronic format, either online or on a CD-ROM. Or you can ask your financial advisor for help in projecting your costs.

THE PRACTICAL RETIREMENT WORKSHEET

Current age	50
Retirement age	65
Current annual income	$75,000
Annual inflation rate	3%
Annual income needed	$93,478.04
Current retirement assets	$250,000
Additional annual contribution	$7,500
Annual rate of return	8%
Value at retirement	$809,333.55
Annual income at retirement	$64,746.68
Monthly income-Social Security	$1,200
Monthly income-pensions	$1,200
Total annual retirement income	$93,546.68

FACTORS TO CONSIDER

As you prepare a retirement budget, you'll want to take these factors into account:

If you retire at 65, you can expect to live until you're 82½.

At current rates, the cost of living will increase by approximately 75% in those 17½ years.

You have to anticipate changes in Social Security in the future, which means you may get less income from that source.

You can't predict the level of healthcare coverage that your employer will provide after you retire.

There's a direct relationship between age and health costs: About 9% of Americans between ages 65 and 69 need help in handling the tasks of everyday living. But by age 85 almost 50% do. Nursing home stays also increase.

LOOKING AT THE FUTURE

The most revealing thing that projecting your future needs will tell you is how much you will have to add to your retirement accounts each year to produce the income you need to maintain a comfortable life. In the example above, the assumption is that you're able to put away 10% of your current annual income.

Projecting future needs also emphasizes how important the rate of return is in building your retirement assets. In some time periods, when investment markets are depressed, you may not be able to achieve an adequate growth rate. But in periods of strong growth, when it's possible to achieve a return of 8% or more by choosing equity investments, most experts agree that it's risky to settle for less.

Coordinating Your Finances

You want a predictable flow of income, not a juggling act.

If you don't want to scale back your plans for retirement, you must be able to afford them. That starts with making investments before you retire so that the income is available as you need it. The second and equally important part of the job is managing the income so your financial life runs smoothly.

ALL IN THE TIMING

There's a big difference between a regular source of income—such as a Social Security check that's direct-deposited in your account each month— and income that's less predictable or even unexpected, like an inheritance. Extra money can come in handy, but you can't depend on it to pay your bills.

But if you've planned ahead, your investments can play an important part in providing additional regular income to offset predictable costs—the ones that are due every month or quarter.

You can get regular income from investments in several ways, based on the kinds you own. Some, like bonds, pay interest on a regular, predictable schedule. You can also set up a system of regular withdrawals from various accounts, or use cash to buy an immediate annuity, which can provide fixed or variable income paid out in regular, usually monthly, installments for a specific period of time, or for your lifetime, or for two lifetimes.

ADDING UP THE INCOME

The big question is whether your combined sources of income will produce enough money, year in and year out, for as long as you need it. The answer is that they can, if your **return**, or profit on those investments, is significantly greater than the rate of inflation. This way, your investments continue to grow in value at the same time that they're providing you with income.

For example, several well-known companies, including General Electric and Pfizer, have paid dividend income to shareholders for years while the value of the shares has fluctuated. If you owned enough shares, you could count on the quarterly dividend payments to cover your predictable costs, even as those costs increased with inflation.

On the other hand, growth rates aren't predictable and dividends aren't guaranteed. So there may be periods of time when income and growth slows. That's why experts caution it's essential to own a variety of investments, including some that guarantee a steady, if less than spectacular, rate of return.

ANNUITY PAYMENTS

WINDFALLS

STOCK DIVIDENDS

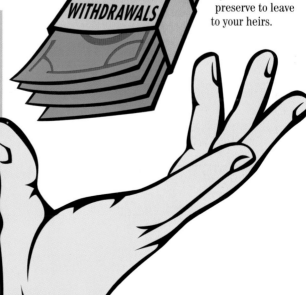

MANAGING YOUR INCOME

If you have a varied portfolio of investments in place as you approach retirement, you'll make out best if you know how to tap them in the most productive ways. Here are some of the things to consider:

- Learn the difference between investments designed to be depleted, or used up in your lifetime, and those better suited to building an estate

- Create a withdrawal schedule to ensure that your assets last as long as you need them, usually for your estimated lifetime and perhaps your spouse's estimated lifetime as well

- Compare the tax consequences of different types of withdrawals so you get to keep more and pay Uncle Sam less over the years

PLAN AHEAD

One way to manage your budget to cover large but anticipated expenses, such as a new car or a new roof, is to funnel a portion of each month's total income into a special money market or savings account. You can use the same method to accumulate money for property taxes or insurance bills.

DEPLETE OR PRESERVE?

Deliberately spending money so there's nothing left when you die makes a lot of sense—if you're not running through your assets so fast that you end up short. Depleting your resources is the principle on which mandatory withdrawals from certain tax-deferred investments is based. For example, the government requires you to set up withdrawals from your IRAs so you're using up those assets during your lifetime. Making regular withdrawals from your annuities, which are also designed as retirement income programs, works the same way.

In contrast, you can invest to build your estate, which means preserving rather than depleting your assets. You're free to leave your taxable investments untouched if you don't need the money, or you may choose to withdraw some of the earnings while leaving the principal to grow. Of course, there's nothing to stop you from investing both ways, building some accounts you intend to deplete to subsidize your retirement and others you intend to preserve to leave to your heirs.

19

Strategies for Living

There are different approaches to spending money in retirement.

How should you use the assets you've accumulated to make your retirement as comfortable and rewarding as you want it to be? The answer depends, in part, on what your attitude toward spending money is.

Experts frequently comment on three categories of retirement spenders:

- Those who live on their earnings only, trying never to use any of the **principal**, or amount they invested

- Those who plan to spend all their money, both principal and earnings, while they are alive, which is sometimes described as **total liquidation**

- Those who earmark portions of their retirement nest egg for certain expenses, which is also described as selective allocation or creating **mental accounts**

Specific retirement investments are better suited for one spending style than others. The smartest move, assuming that you've accumulated a diversified retirement account with a range of investments, is to match the way you use each type with the way it can serve you best.

THE PRINCIPAL IS THE BASIS OF MY SECURITY.

Spend the interest while preserving the principal

PRESERVE THE PRINCIPAL

There's real logic in trying to preserve principal. It's principal, after all, that produces earnings in your investment accounts year after year, and that growth forms the basis of your security. When the principal disappears, there's nothing left to accumulate earnings.

On the other hand, assets left when you die are assets you didn't enjoy. Some of them can be passed to your heirs through your will or different types of trusts, or become their property as the result of your naming them as beneficiaries. Those assets may be taxed.

You have no choice about whether to preserve or spend in certain cases: Pensions are paid out on a fixed schedule and, in most cases, you're required by law to withdraw from your traditional IRAs, SEPs, and similar plans once you've reached 70½. But with other investments, you can postpone withdrawing until age 85 or later, and in some cases never touch them at all.

THE IMPACT OF TAXES

Most experts suggest you'll want to take taxes into account when you're deciding which assets to use for income in retirement, assuming you have a variety from which to choose. That's because what your heirs will owe varies with different types of inherited investments.

Stocks, for example, become the property of your heirs at their current market value. No tax is ever due on the gains that occurred prior to your death.

Investments in IRAs, annuities, and other tax-deferred investments are taxed as they are withdrawn. The timing of those withdrawals, and taxes that are due, depends on the way your particular plan is set up. If you're married, your spouse can spread them over his or her lifetime, and the same may be true for other beneficiaries as well. That's one of the provisions to check as you choose among tax-deferred investments.

SETTING PRIORITIES

The things most people consider important uses of their money in retirement are:

- Meeting their own and their spouse's needs (food, medical care, lodging)
- Having money to do the things they enjoy, such as travel, leisure activities or whatever appeals
- Providing for their heirs
- Making charitable contributions

I EARNED IT—I'LL SPEND IT!

ONE FOR THIS, AND ONE FOR THAT...

Spend down your savings year by year

Spend from different accounts for different purposes

| Account 1 | Account 2 |
| Account 3 | Account 4 |

SPEND IT ALL

Your attitude toward the assets you've accumulated may well be "I earned it, I'll spend it." Lots of people share that view, and with good reason. The point of accumulating retirement assets is, after all, your ability to live a rich and fulfilling life for 20, 30 or more years after you stop working.

Although the idea of spending all your retirement money may seem reckless, the truth is that most retirement plans are set up for precisely that reason. An annuitization plan, which you can choose for your pension or annuity payout, promises to pay out your accumulated assets over a set period of years, or for your lifetime or your and your spouse's joint lifetimes.

In other cases, you can use up the assets as you please, turning them into cash at whatever pace you like. The danger, of course, is using up your assets while you're still around to need them.

MENTAL ACCOUNTS

If you analyze the way you think about money, you may find that you allocate your assets into distinct categories in your head. You may, for example, put the money you spend on living expenses in one category, what you've got set aside for retirement in another, and your investment assets in a third—and you don't mix and match.

A simple example is earmarking your bonus to pay for a special family vacation. Someone who practices the principle of mental accounting wouldn't sell off an investment or borrow the money from a retirement plan to take a vacation, but would be comfortable assigning extra income to that use.

If handling money that way makes sense to you, you'll be likely to use mental accounting in retirement as well. That can position you to identify which investments you should use for living expenses, which for special expenses, and which for preserving in your estate.

The Last Paycheck

Retiring means stitching together different sources of income.

When you retire, you'll share a common experience with everyone who has already made the change: You won't get a paycheck anymore.

Without this steady stream of revenue, you'll have to arrange for the income you'll need to live. Specifically, you'll need to consider the following:

- What sources of income are you confident you can count on?

- How much income will they provide each year?

- How and when will the income be paid?

- How will you coordinate payments from different sources to create a steady stream of income, so that there's money in the bank when you need it?

WHAT THE SOURCES ARE

You'll probably count on income from a number of different sources.

Social Security income is paid to people who contribute to the system, and to their dependents.

Pensions provide income from a retirement plan your employer has established in your name.

Salary reduction plans let you use pretax salary to build an investment portfolio. Assets can be withdrawn to provide income.

IRAs are Individual Retirement Accounts that let your investments grow tax-deferred until you begin regular withdrawals, usually after age 59½.

Annuities are tax-deferred investment contracts that can be converted to a regular stream of income, which will continue throughout your lifetime.

Personal investments in stocks, bonds, mutual funds, real estate, CDs, and other products can provide retirement income, be converted to cash or be used to buy income-producing investments, including annuities.

Jobs, either part-time or full-time, can provide income as you need it.

WHEN THE MONEY ARRIVES

Unlike a paycheck, which arrives regularly, retirement income arrives on different schedules. Social Security checks and annuity and pension payments usually come monthly. Others, like stock dividends, arrive quarterly. Interest on bonds is paid semi-annually. Few, if any payments, are weekly or bi-weekly. That means you have to think about balancing the amount coming in to meet your expenses.

PUTTING IT TOGETHER

Managing your finances during retirement involves juggling your sources of income to make sure you have enough money to live on. It's a lot like making a quilt: No piece by itself is big enough to keep you warm at night. But properly stitched together, the pieces can provide a lot of comfort.

THE INCOME THEY'LL PROVIDE

The amount of income you'll receive from Social Security and a pension depends on your work history and, with some pensions, on the investment choices you make. In most cases, the longer you work and the higher your salary, the more income you can anticipate. On the other hand, tax-deferred retirement plans (including salary-reduction plans), IRAs, and variable annuities produce income in relation to the amounts you put into them and the investment choices you make.

The average retired person gets 40% of his or her retirement income from Social Security, 20% from investment assets, 20% from employer pensions, and 18% from continuing employment, according to research conducted by the Employee Benefit Research Institute and the National Academy on Aging. In the future, though, there's consensus among retirement experts that employer pensions and Social Security will provide less. That means personal investment assets are going to play a much larger role for most people.

INVESTMENTS BUT NOT INCOME—YET

Though you may have substantial net worth, not all of your investments may produce income. Growth stocks have value but don't give you access to cash until you sell them or use them as collateral to borrow. And unless you have thousands of shares, even stocks that pay regular dividends rarely provide enough money to live on.

If your primary real estate investment is your home, it won't produce income either. You can probably arrange a reverse mortgage, or loan against your equity, but unless you're quite old the amount will be relatively small. What's more, you'll be reducing your equity every time you draw on it.

An alternative is to shift your assets gradually into investments that produce income either through annuitization—a regular payout from an annuity investment—or a systematic withdrawal arrangement.

What you need to make the best use of your investment assets is a plan for producing the income you need and a strategy to make it happen.

Social Security

Security means knowing there's money coming in every month.

If retirement and Social Security seem one and the same to you, there's good reason. More than 90% of U.S. households with someone over 65 are part of the system. And their monthly benefits check is the primary source of income for almost 67% of those households.

Since its introduction in 1935, in the wake of the Great Depression, Social Security has evolved from a safety net designed to relieve poverty to the mainstay of a secure retirement. But the role it will play for future generations is less certain. Fewer workers will be putting money into the system in the 21st century while more will be collecting benefits.

WHAT YOU CONTRIBUTE

If you're in the Social Security system—and more than 96% of the workforce is—you currently contribute 7.65% of your salary every year, 6.2% for retirement and disability benefits and 1.45% for Medicare coverage. Your employer contributes an equal amount, and if you're self-employed you pay both shares. There's an annual cap on contributions for retirement and disability—it's $5,263.80 in 2002, or 6.2% of $84,900—but no cap on Medicare contributions.

The 6.2% retirement deduction stops when you reach the cap ($84,900 in 2002)

The 1.45% Medicare deduction never stops

LOOKING AT THE NUMBERS
According to recent statistics, there are 3.4 people working—and putting money into the system— for every retired person. That's a far cry from 1950, when there were 16 workers for every retired person. By 2030, that number is expected to decrease to 2.1 workers for every retired person.

Where You Stand

Your Social Security Earnings

Years	Social Security		
	Maximum Taxable Earnings	Your Reported Earnings	Estimated Taxes You Paid
1990	51,300	51,300	3,180
1991	53,400	53,400	3,310
1992	55,500	38,267	2,372
1993	57,600	57,600	3,571
1994	60,600	60,600	3,757
1995	61,200	61,200	3,794
1996	62,700	62,700	3,887
1997	65,400	65,400	4,054
1998	68,400	68,400	4,240
1999	72,600	72,600	4,501
2000	76,200	76,200	4,274
2001	80,400	80,400	4,984

You put money into Social Security each year you receive reported income

Your contribution is figured on all of your income up to the amount of the annual cap

There's an annual cap on the amount of income that's taxed for Social Security

HOW YOU QUALIFY
You qualify for Social Security benefits in two steps:

- You contribute to the Social Security system, usually with money your employer withholds from your salary
- You accumulate 40 credits during the years you work. You can get up to four credits a year, one for each time you earn the minimum required for that year. For 2002, that amount was $870

So a person who earns $3,500 a year and a person who earns $100,000 a year each accumulates four credits. If you work full time, you'll be fully qualified in ten years, but you'll also qualify if you gain the credits more sporadically.

However, the benefits you receive depend more on the amount you contribute to the system than on simply accumulating the credits to qualify.

FIGURING BENEFITS

The formula the Social Security Administration (SSA) uses to calculate your primary insurance amount (PIA)—the base on which your benefit is figured—is designed to give you credit for your 35 highest paying years, thereby increasing the amount you'll receive.

Here's how it works:

1. Your lifetime earnings (to age 60) are adjusted for inflation, so they're counted at their current value.

2. Your total earnings are divided by the number of months you worked, to find what's known as your average indexed monthly earnings.

3. Your permanent base benefit is figured on your average indexed monthly earnings.

Generally speaking, the more you've contributed, the larger your monthly benefit. In 2002, for example, the average benefit for a single person at age 65 is $848, but a person at the top of the scale receives $1,660.

Retirement

If you retire at 62, your monthly benefit in today's dollars will be about . . . . $ 975

The earliest age at which you can receive an unreduced retirement benefit is 65 and 10 months. We call this your full retirement age. If you wait until that age to receive benefits, your monthly benefit in today's dollars will be about . . . . $ 1,325

If you wait until you are 70 to receive benefits, your monthly benefit in today's dollars will be about . . . . $ 1,790

You contribute 6.2% of your income until you reach the maximum required contribution. Then no more taxes are withheld

You can get an estimate of the benefit you will receive if you retire at full retirement age, at age 62 or if you wait until age 70

WHERE YOU STAND

The SSA will tell you what you've paid in, and give you an estimate of what you can expect to receive when you retire. You'll receive an updated Social Security Statement each year about three months before your birthday. And you can request a copy at any time by visiting the Social Security website at www.ssa.gov.

You should review your updated statement carefully to be sure your records are correct. If you find an error—which can happen if you've had more than one employer, for example—you can send the SSA copies of the relevant W-2 forms and have the mistake corrected. The sooner you uncover a problem, the more easily it can be corrected.

The information on your Social Security Statement also helps with your financial planning. If you know what you can expect each month from Social Security, you've got a much better sense of what you'll need from other sources.

YOU HAVE TO APPLY

You don't get your benefits automatically. You have to apply to the SSA, and the time to begin is in the year before you plan to retire. One reason to plan ahead is that you may be able to adjust your start date and increase the overall amount of your benefits.

TAXES ON BENEFITS

Whether it seems fair or not, you may have to pay tax on part of your Social Security benefits, reducing the amount you'll have available to live on. That happens when your total income for the year, including half your Social Security payment, is more than the levels set by Congress.

What's even more surprising is that you might find yourself in this situation even if your income seems modest. That's because the income limits are relatively low and practically all of your income is counted, even earnings on tax-exempt investments.

Filing Status	Income Level	
Single	$25,000	$34,000
Married, living apart with separate returns	$25,000	$34,000
Married	$32,000	$44,000
Married, filing separately	any income	
Amount of benefit taxed	**50%**	**85%**

The Benefits You Get

The big question with benefits is when to start.

Perhaps the biggest decision you'll have to make about Social Security is when to start collecting your benefits. SSA adjusts what you get based on your age as one way of trying to equalize what people receive over their lifetimes.

You can take a reduced benefit at 62, wait until you're eligible to receive your full benefit, or postpone your first payment to qualify for a larger amount. Most experts advise you to start your benefit as soon as you're retired and no later than 70, since there's no bonus for waiting longer than that.

THE DIFFERENCE AGE MAKES

You're eligible to collect the full benefit you qualify for at age 65 provided you were born in 1937 or before. If you were born later, you'll have to be a little older. Check the chart below for the age that applies to you. But don't be surprised if you're required to be at least 70 for full benefits before too long. That's one proposal for preserving the system into the 21st century.

Whose Benefits?

If you and your spouse are both eligible for benefits based on your work histories, you'll have to decide whether to draw on your accounts individually, or have one of you collect spousal benefits.

If the total you'd receive by each drawing on your own accounts is less than 150% of what either one of you would qualify for on your own, it doesn't make sense to collect individually. That's because the person with the lower benefit can collect as a dependent spouse, which adds 50% to the larger benefit. When the spouse with the higher benefit dies, the survivor qualifies for that larger base amount.

For example, if you qualified for $1,352 and your spouse for $600, you'd receive $76 a month more with the dependent benefit than if you collected separately. If your spouse qualified for $800, you'd be better off taking individual benefits, for the added $124 a month.

Changes in Social Security Retirement-Age Provisions

Year of Birth	Attainment of Age 62	Starting Age for Full Benefits (Year/Months)	Credit for Each Year of Delayed Retirement	Age-62 Benefit as % of PIA
1938	2000	65/2	6.5%	79.2%
1939	2001	65/4	7.0%	78.3%
1940	2002	65/6	7.0%	77.5%
1941	2003	65/8	7.5%	76.7%
1942	2004	65/10	7.5%	75.8%
1943-54	2005-16	66/0	8.0%	75.0%
1955	2017	66/2	8.0%	74.2%
1956	2018	66/4	8.0%	73.3%
1957	2019	66/6	8.0%	72.5%
1958	2020	66/8	8.0%	71.7%
1959	2021	66/10	8.0%	70.8%
1960+	2022+	67/0	8.0%	70.0%

DIVORCED PARTNERS RIGHTS

Even if you are divorced, you may still be eligible to collect benefits based on your former spouse's earnings record. If you were married for at least ten years, have not re-married, and are not eligible for equal or larger benefits based on another person's benefits, you should qualify.

The amount you get doesn't reduce what your former mate (and his or her new spouse) receives.

If over 35 years you paid **$59,619** to Social Security and collected benefits for 20 years, you'd get at least **$318,000**

WHAT'S IN STORE?

Currently you get Social Security benefits based on what you paid into the system. But one proposal for keeping the program in the black would impose **means testing**. In that case your right to collect benefits would be tied to your overall income. The more you had from other sources, the less you'd be eligible for from Social Security. Will that happen? There's no way to be sure. But it certainly could.

If you die, your surviving spouse gets the full amount of your benefit (including the COLAs) for life. In this example, that would be $1,352, the same amount you'd receive if you were the survivor.

If you have questions about your benefits, such as when to begin, whether to collect as a spouse, or how to change a decision you've already made, an SSA staff person can help you.

FIRST FIGURE SPOUSAL BENEFIT

Higher of the two benefits	$1,352
50% of the higher benefit	+ 676
Total spousal benefit	=$2,028

THEN COMPARE YOUR INDIVIDUAL BENEFITS

Example A

Higher of the two benefits	$1,352
Spouse's benefit	+ 600
Total benefit	=$1,952

If the lower of the benefits is **less** than 50% of the higher, **take the spousal benefit**

Example B

Higher of the two benefits	$1,352
Spouse's benefit	+ 800
Total benefit	=$2,152

If the lower of the benefits is **more** than 50% of the higher, **collect individually**

A GROWING BENEFIT

Unlike many retirement plans, Social Security benefits are increased regularly to account for inflation. You get a **cost of living adjustment**, or **COLA**, each year after you begin to collect. Your COLA is figured by multiplying the annual percentage of increase by the base amount of your benefit.

For example, for 2002, benefits went up 2.6%. That means a monthly benefit of $1,000 in 2001 increased to $1,026 in 2002. The rate of increase differs from year to year: It's greater in periods of high inflation and smaller in periods of low inflation. But your benefits never decrease.

The COLAs begin when you're 62 even if you don't start collecting. Their accumulated value is added to your base amount when you do begin to receive benefits. That means the checks you receive will be larger and your future COLAs will be figured on the higher base.

Cost of Living

COLA (Cost of Living Adjustment)

INVESTMENT DEBATE

The money that's withheld from your salary plus an equal amount from your employer goes into two Social Security trust funds, which invest in U.S. Treasury bonds, where they earn the current rate of interest.

Critics of that investment approach argue that the system isn't benefiting from the growth that can come from investing in equities. They advocate allocating at least a portion of the trust funds to the stock market or to mutual funds investing in the market.

Another proposed solution, though controversial, would allow Social Security participants to invest a portion of their annual contribution as they chose. The argument is that if people put money into equities, they could boost the amount of their long-term income. Those opposed argue that the plan could jeopardize the ability of the system to provide a safety net for the neediest recipients. And they fear that many people would lack the confidence to invest in ways likely to benefit them the most.

Pensions

You get regular retirement income from a
pension—if you have one.

Some employers reward employees for the
years they work by providing pensions
after they retire. There are two basic
types of pensions, traditional
defined benefit plans and the
newer **defined contribution plans**.

HOW THE PENSIONS WORK

The key difference between a defined
benefit plan and a defined **contribution** plan boils down to this: With
defined benefit, you're guaranteed a lifetime income based
on a specific formula. With
defined contribution, your
retirement income depends
on the investment perfor-
mance of the amounts that
are contributed.

While there is more
potential for in-
creased retirement
income than there is
with a defined benefit
plan, there is no
income guarantee.

That makes it
harder to know how
much income you'll
need to provide from
other sources.

There are some
other differences too.
Some (though not all) defined contribution plans are **self-directed**,
which means you decide how to
invest the amount your employer
contributes each year. That
amount may be linked to how
profitable your employer has
been in the last year.

There are resemblances
between defined benefit and
defined contribution plans as
well. With both, the employer
makes the contribution and
administers the plan. The
amounts contributed don't
increase your current taxable salary, or decrease it
as salary reduction plans
like 401(k)s do. Finally, all
full-time employees are
eligible to participate,
though in a defined
contribution plan they
can decline to do so.

**YOUR
EMPLOYER
ADDS MONEY
to retirement
accounts set up
in your name
and gets a tax
deduction for
the amount.**

**With a defined contribution
plan, you can't predict what
your pension income will be
because the amount depends on
how much is contributed to the
plan and the way it is invested.**

CORPORATE PENSIONS

Companies aren't
required to establish
pension plans, but
many do. The
promise of long-
term security
can make a job
appealing to po-
tential workers,
which helps an em-
ployer in recruiting
and maintaining staff
over time. When some
employees have pension
rights negotiated by their
union, the company often
provides pensions for other
workers as well.

Pensions also provide
financial benefits for employers, who
can deduct the money they pay into pension plans from their corporate taxes. But
the government monitors and regulates
these plans, making them expensive to
administer. That's one reason many small
companies don't offer them, and why
some large companies have ended
their plans.

The result is that many more people
are responsible for providing retirement
income on their own.

A BRIEF PENSION HISTORY

Military pensions for U.S. soldiers go back to
the American Revolution. American Express
introduced the first corporate pension in 1875,
and in the 1920s the federal government
introduced public employee pensions.

Corporate pensions grew in popularity
after the Great Depression, a result of the
specter of widespread poverty among the
elderly and a growing union movement. And
pension plans got a big boost in the 1940s,
when pay raises were illegal, so employers
promised retirement income to attract and
keep their workers.

A DIVIDABLE ASSET
If you divorce, your pension assets will be probably be divided,
especially if you've been married
a long time.

With a defined benefit plan, you'll know before you retire how much income you'll receive. It may be paid either in regular amounts over your lifetime or as a one-time lump sum.

HITTING THE TOP

There are limits to what pensions can provide. If you have a defined benefit pension, the annual income you receive after you retire is typically capped at 100% of your average annual salary for the years you worked for that employer, or the cap may be a fixed dollar amount adjusted annually for inflation. In 2002, the maximum pension payout is $160,000. That amount will increase in $5,000 increments to reflect increases in inflation.

With a defined contribution plan, your employer may be able to contribute up to 100% of your salary, to a specific dollar cap. For 2002, the upper limit is $40,000, scheduled to increase in $1,000 increments to keep pace with inflation.

GOVERNMENT PENSIONS

Government pensions, which have been a major attraction to people working in the public sector, differ from corporate pensions in several ways.

- Government employees are often required to contribute a percentage of their after-tax earnings to their pensions.

- Government employees can receive their pensions after a set period of time—such as 20 or 30 years—no matter how old they are or how close they are to normal retirement age.

- Government pensions are automatically adjusted for inflation using a cost of living index adjustment, or COLA.

VESTING

If you have a pension, you need to know about vesting. It's the amount of time you must work at a company before you're eligible to collect your pension. Typically, a private company employee becomes fully vested—or entitled to full benefits of the employer pension—after five years of service, or an employee may be gradually vested between years three and seven. A public employee, however, may have to be on the job ten years or longer.

If you leave a job before you're vested, you may give up your rights to the pension, or may be eligible for only a fraction of the potential benefit. That's one handicap of constantly changing jobs: You may never qualify for a pension, or at best you'll receive a number of modest payments from several different employers.

If you are vested and leave a job, your benefits may be frozen at the time you leave and simply sit there until you eventually retire. In other cases, your account continues to grow, which will provide you with a larger pension. Or, you may have to move the assets to a different plan or an IRA.

YOUR PENSION ACCOUNT grows tax deferred, and you owe no taxes until you begin receiving income after retirement.

SUPPORTING YOUR SPOUSE

If you're married and belong to a defined benefit plan, your employer is legally bound to pay at least 50% of your pension amount to your surviving spouse when you die. You can choose a different payout option, which might mean you'd receive a larger amount in your lifetime, but your spouse must sign a written consent waiving rights to the income.

Most experts believe that it makes sense to protect your spouse with this life-time payment, unless he or she has a good pension plan as well. One alternative may be to buy a life insurance policy in combination with a single life annuity, sometimes called a pension maximization plan, to provide income for a surviving spouse.

Defined Benefit Pensions

If there's a good old plan, this is it.

If you're part of a defined benefit pension plan, your employer puts money into a retirement fund in your name, chooses the investments the fund makes, and handles all the administrative details, including making the payments.

PENSION ANNUITY

Typically a pension is paid in regular installments over your lifetime. What you get is known as a pension annuity.

Pluses
- Choice of payout models
- Income to last your lifetime and your spouse's lifetime
- Insurance to cover at least part of income through the Pension Benefit Guarantee Corporation

Minuses
- Vulnerability to inflation
- Taxes due on each payment at your regular income tax rate
- Risk of under-funding or plan termination by your employer

WHAT YOU GET

Defined benefit means that you get a specific amount of money when you retire. The amount is determined by a formula set out in the plan itself. Generally, it factors in your final salary, the number of years you worked at the job, and your age when you retire. Some plans may provide as much as 30% to 50% of your final salary at the standard retirement age of 65. There's no law, though, that commits your employer to paying a specific percentage or dollar amount.

If you retire early, you'll probably receive less than you would have been eligible for at 65. If you work longer, the amount should be larger since you'll benefit from added contributions. If you're relying on your pension for a big chunk of your retirement income, you'll probably want to take those factors into account.

INCOME OPTIONS

When you're ready to start collecting your pension, you'll often have a choice about how to take your money. To figure out what's best, you have to consider how much regular income you'll need, the other income sources you can count on, and the tax implications of your choices.

You should be able to get advice from your human resources office, but you'll probably also want to discuss your options with your tax and financial advisors since your decision will have an impact on other areas of your financial life.

Remember: You can't change your mind. Once you've made a pension payout decision, there's no going back.

TIME PAYS

Defined benefit pensions reward time on the job. Employers frequently calculate the amount you'll get by multiplying the years you've worked by .015, and then multiplying the result by your final salary. Based on this formula, the number of years you work can have a bigger impact

ROLLOVER

You move your pension fund directly into a designated IRA or annuity if your employer's plan offers a lump-sum distribution option.

Pluses

- Continued tax-deferred growth
- Control over investment decisions
- Flexible withdrawal amounts

Minuses

- Taxes on withdrawal amounts at your regular income-tax rate
- Must begin withdrawing by age 70½

Corporate pensions and most pensions provided by educational, medical, and other not-for-profit institutions are rarely indexed for inflation. Unlike Social Security, where your benefit increases every year, your pension amount is likely to be set in stone.

That's one reason people sometimes choose a payout option that lets them invest for growth, using mutual funds, variable annuities or direct stock purchases.

PERIODIC PAYMENTS

Your employer will pay you the amount of your pension in regular payments over a fixed period, typically 5 to 15 years.

Pluses

- Regular payments at regular intervals
- Larger monthly payments
- Flexibility to invest
- Some amounts eligible for IRA rollover

Minuses

- No access to lump sum amount
- No guarantee of lifetime income
- Taxes due on each payment at regular income tax rate

LUMP SUM

Your employer makes a cash payment of all the money in your pension fund.

Pluses

- Control over your money
- Ability to invest as you choose
- Option to forward average taxes if you were born before 1936

Minuses

- Substantial tax due
- No guarantee of lifetime income
- Increased responsibility for managing finances

INTEGRATED PLANS

Integrated plans are pensions with a wrinkle. These plans count some of your Social Security income as part of your defined benefit, and reduce the pension amount you receive. While this policy may seem unfair, it's legal because it recognizes that your employer contributed half of your Social Security taxes. So it pays to check if you're part of such a plan. If you are, you'll have an even greater incentive to build an investment portfolio that will help make up the difference.

A CHANGING LANDSCAPE

Defined benefit plans are less common than they once were, as employers move away from the practice of providing guaranteed retirement income. One reason may be the complex rules that can make administering such a plan difficult.

In addition, some existing pension contracts are being renegotiated, so that new employees will be eligible to receive less at retirement and will qualify at a later age. In addition, some traditional ways of boosting final salary to increase pension amounts, such as extra overtime and across-the-board cost of living increases, are being eliminated.

on your pension amount than your final salary. For example, if your final salary were $55,000 after 30 years on the job, you'd get a bigger pension—$24,750 a year—than a co-worker earning $72,000 who'd been there 20 years—$21,600.

A few years before your actual retirement date, you should be able to get an estimate of the amount you'll receive by asking your employer. Though you might get an additional raise, you can be fairly confident that the final amount won't be less than the estimate.

THE INFLATION DILEMMA

One of the biggest problems with defined benefit pensions is that when the fixed payouts stretch over a retired person's lifetime or a husband and wife's joint lifetime, they're vulnerable to inflation.

Defined Contribution Plans

Good intentions can produce great results—but there's no guarantee.

If you're part of a defined contribution plan, your employer adds money to your retirement account, but doesn't make any promises about the income you'll receive after you stop working. The annual contribution amount is determined by the specific type of plan your employer provides.

WHAT YOU'LL GET

The benefits you'll receive from a defined contribution plan depend on:

- The amount that's contributed, which often varies from year to year and may even be skipped entirely in some years

- How well the investments perform

For example, if the investments are in equities, and the stock market is strong, your account could grow substantially. But if the economy is sluggish or if the investments in your name falter, the growth of your account could be slowed.

In most cases, the money that goes into the plan is in addition to your salary, and you owe no income tax on the amount your employer contributes. However, you will owe tax on the money you eventually receive in pension payments.

PORTABILITY

Defined contribution plans often offer the benefit of portability—the ability to transfer your accumulated assets from one plan to another. Or you can roll them over into an IRA trust or an Individual Retirement Annuity.

If you can't transfer your account to a new employer, either because there's no plan where you've moved or the money is invested in stock in your former company, you can sometimes leave the account in your former employer's plan. Unlike the assets in a defined benefit plan you leave behind, money in defined contribution plans has the potential to grow until you are ready to retire.

EMPLOYEE STOCK OWNERSHIP PLANS (ESOP)

With an ESOP, your employer contributes stock in the company to your plan, or subsidizes your purchase of the stock. The advantage of an ESOP is the chance to share in company profits, and to accumulate a substantial holding over time. The downside is that all your eggs are in one basket. If your company has financial trouble, both your job and your retirement money could be in jeopardy. However, experts advise you to take advantage of an ESOP if it's offered, since the benefits of growth potential outweigh the risks.

MONEY PURCHASE PLANS

Money purchase plans are the most generous of the defined contribution plans because they let your employer contribute the highest amounts allowed by law to your retirement account. The cap is a percentage of your salary, up to the annual limit. The only drawback, from your employer's perspective, is that once a commitment to a specific percentage is made, the same level of contribution has to be made each year, whether the company is doing well or not.

Retirement

PAYOUT OPTIONS

There are fewer payout options with defined contribution plans:

- The assets may be sold and distributed to you as a lump sum. In that case, you are responsible for investing the entire amount

GETTING THE TERMS STRAIGHT

Sometimes salary reduction plans, such as 401(k)s, 403(b)s (TSAs), and various government plans to which you contribute part of your salary, are also described as defined contribution plans. But those plans aren't described as pensions, since your retirement income is provided by reducing your current salary. What's important, though, is understanding how the different plans work.

PROFIT SHARING PLANS

With profit sharing, your employer contributes a percentage of the company's total profits into your retirement account. In good years, the amount can be substantial. But in a poor year, it might be nothing, since your employer isn't obligated to contribute every year.

One advantage of profit sharing over other defined contribution plans is that you may be able to borrow against the amount accumulated in your account.

As with a money purchase plan, profit sharing is one of the options open to the owner of a very small company, including one with a single employee.

SEPS

A Simplified Employee Pension, or SEP, is an IRA set up in your name by your employer, who may contribute a percentage of your salary every year up to the annual limit. You decide how the money is invested, which gives you added control over your finances.

You can roll over your SEP-IRA into a rollover IRA if you change jobs.

The downside can be that your employer may change the amount of the contribution every year or even skip some years. You won't have any control over that.

If you own a small company, you can set up a SEP even if you're the only employee.

SIMPLES

Savings Incentive Match Plans for Employees are a new breed of defined contribution plans. Like salary reduction plans, a SIMPLE lets you contribute up to the annual limit of your pretax salary if you want to participate in the plan. Your employer must contribute. The amount of your employer's contribution is set by one of two formulas, either 3% of the salary of each participating employee or 2% of the salary of every employee. The money that's contributed goes into an IRA in your name, and you choose the investments. One drawback of these plans is that the withdrawal rules are stricter than other plans.

Account

- Some employers offer annuity contracts, allowing you to convert your assets into a stream of income to be paid out over your lifetime, and sometimes your spouse's lifetime

- If you participate in a stock ownership plan, you can hold onto the stock or sell it and reinvest the money

CHANGING NUMBERS

The amount your employer can contribute to a defined contribution plan in your name will increase gradually between 2002 and 2006 to reflect increases in inflation. For example, if inflation increases at an annual rate of 3%, the contribution ceiling will increase $1,000 a year—to $41,000 in 2003 and to $45,000 by 2006.

Similarly, the amount you can contribute to a SIMPLE plan will increase in $1,000 increments from $7,000 in 2002 to $10,000 in 2005.

Salary Reduction Plans

You can reduce your taxes and invest for retirement at the same time.

If you want to invest for retirement, the first thing to check is whether your employer offers a salary reduction plan. These varieties of defined contribution plans are hard to beat in terms of their convenience, tax savings, and opportunity to provide long-term growth.

HOW SALARY REDUCTION PLANS WORK

With a salary reduction plan, you put money into an account set up through your employer and usually administered by a brokerage firm, a mutual fund company or other financial institution. The amount you contribute and the earnings in your account are not taxed until you start withdrawing the money, usually at retirement.

Some plans also allow you to contribute after-tax dollars. This option may be a good way to add extra savings to your retirement plan, but you may be better off making other tax-deferred investments to take advantage of their tax benefits and get more flexibility at the same time. It's a good idea to check with your financial advisor about the best option for you.

PICKING INVESTMENTS

Salary reduction plans are typically **self-directed**, which means you choose how and where your money is invested. The specific choices you have depend on the plan, but typically you can choose from a mix of investments, including annuities, mutual funds, fixed-income investments, and company stock.

LOWER TAXES

Because you contribute to your plan on a pretax basis, the amount you put in is not reported to the IRS on your W-2. That reduces your taxable income—and your take-home salary—for the year. For example, if you earned $50,000 and contributed $5,000 to your company's plan, your employer would report you had a taxable income of $45,000.

Your salary	**$50,000**
Plan contribution	**– 5,000**
YOUR TAXABLE SALARY	**= $45,000**

If you have a broad choice of investments, you should compare their specific objectives and their performance records before choosing among them. You can get information from the mutual fund companies or annuity providers directly, and you can find reports and analysis in financial magazines and the financial pages of big city newspapers. Most experts advise you to put most of your salary reduction account in equity investments. Alternatives that may seem safer may not produce enough growth to offset inflation and the eventual tax you'll owe.

TYPES OF PLANS

There are a variety of salary reduction plans, each with some distinctive characteristics. The type that's available to you depends on the company or organization you work for.

401(k) plans

401(k) plans are offered by corporations and non-profit organizations, which often match a percentage of your contribution. Your contribution limit for 2002 is $11,000, increasing to $15,000 in 2006. If you're 50 or older, you may also make annual catch-up contributions.

403(b) plans

403(b) plans are available to employees of educational, healthcare, and non-profit, tax-exempt organizations. In 2002, you can contribute up to $11,000. That cap will increase annually to $15,000 in 2006. If you're 50 or older, you may also make annual catch-up contributions.

As you build your retirement assets, you may want to aim for an 11% return each year, the historical average for equities. If it's consistently lower, it may be time to rebalance your accounts.

MATCHING FUNDS

Employers often match a percentage of the amount you contribute to your salary reduction plan. A typical plan might match 50% of what you contribute, up to 6% of your total salary.

Let's say you earn $50,000 and contribute 6% of your salary, or $3,000 a year, to your plan. If the employer matches 50% of your contribution, or $1,500, the total added to the account at year end will be $4,500. But if you contributed 15% of your salary, or $7,500, your employer's contribution would be capped at $3,000 (6% of your salary) rather than at 50% of your contribution, or $3,750.

You Contribute	Employer Contributes
6% = $3,000 of salary	50% = $1,500 of your contribution
15% = $7,500 of salary	Up to 6% of your salary = $3,000

It's also smart to diversify your equity investments by choosing several within the plan, rather than putting all your money into one investment account or mutual fund. That lets you benefit from those that turn in a strong performance and offset potentially weaker returns by others in any given period.

If you want to change your investment mix or rebalance your holdings, most salary reduction plans let you transfer assets among the various choices. You owe no tax on any earnings you transfer, since the plans provide tax-deferred growth.

NO GUARANTEES

Salary reduction plans provide no guarantees on the amount of retirement income you'll receive. That's because any growth in your account depends on the amount you contribute and the performance of your investment accounts. History has shown that equity investments—including those you can make with stock mutual funds and variable annuities—increase in value over the long term, but no promises can be made. In fact, your investment may actually lose money, especially in the short term, because the value of the underlying investments, such as the stocks a fund or annuity invests in, may go down.

WITHDRAWING ASSETS

When you retire, you have a number of withdrawal options. You can roll the assets in your salary reduction plan into an IRA or qualified annuity, where it can continue to grow tax-deferred. You'll have to begin systematic withdrawals or annuitize when you reach age 70½, and you'll owe tax at your regular income tax rates on each withdrawal.

If you prefer, you can take a lump sum payout and reinvest, though you'll owe a lot of tax immediately. With what is left you could buy an immediate annuity, taxable investments such as stocks or bonds, or income-producing, tax-exempt municipal bonds. You can ask your financial advisor to help you figure out if that approach makes sense for you.

It may not be a good idea to put all the money into low-paying accounts that promise safety of principal. They may not keep pace with inflation or provide the income you need to live comfortably.

Section 457 plans

Section 457 plans are designed for employees of state and municipal governments. There's no provision for matching contributions. In 2002, you can contribute up to $11,000. By 2006 that cap will increase to $15,000. If you're 50 or older, you may also make annual catch-up contributions.

Thrift or savings plans

These plans are available to federal employees and to employees of corporations that offer plans. Your employer may match a percentage of your contribution. In the federal plan (FERS) the contribution limit for 2002 is 11% of salary, and in the civil service plan (CERS) it's 6%.

SIMPLE

Savings Incentive Match Plan for Employees, or SIMPLE plans, are designed for employers with 100 or fewer workers who offer no other retirement plans. In 2002, you can contribute up to $7,000, increasing to $10,000 by 2005. If you're 50 or older, you can make catch-up contributions.

Annuities

Annuities can do double duty, as a way to accumulate assets and as personal pensions.

Annuities are retirement plans that you may purchase independently, as **nonqualified plans**, or participate in as part of a **qualified**, employer sponsored program. All **deferred annuities** accumulate any earnings on a tax-deferred basis, at either a fixed or variable rate of return. Both qualified and nonqualified deferred annuities can be converted to a stream of steady retirement income, or the accumulated assets can be used to buy an **immediate annuity** to provide income.

SAVING ON TAXES
In addition to tax-deferred growth of earnings, variable deferred annuities also allow you to move your retirement savings among different investment portfolios without having to pay income tax on any gains. For example, you can move assets from one stock investment portfolio to another offered in the annuity without losing a penny to taxes. That would also be true if you made the transfer within a 401(k) or other qualified retirement plan. You would owe tax, though, if you sold shares in a mutual fund and bought another if those funds weren't held in a tax-deferred retirement plan.

If you want to move your annuity to another annuity with a different company, you can do that without paying any tax on your earnings either. The tax-free transfers are known as 1035 exchanges because they're covered by the section of the federal income tax code with that number.

IMMEDIATE AVAILABILITY
One unique feature of nonqualified annuities is the opportunity to convert a lump sum of cash into an instant pension, or stream of income guaranteed to last your lifetime, or your and your spouse's joint lifetimes.

1. Invest for Retirement

BUILDING YOUR ASSETS
Like other retirement plans, you use an annuity to build your assets over the long-term. A **fixed deferred annuity** promises a set rate of return that's usually guaranteed for an initial period, typically one year. After that, the rate may change. For example, if interest rates in general decline, the annuity provider is likely to reduce the rate at which earnings will be credited to your account. But there's always a guaranteed minimum rate.

With a **variable deferred annuity** you choose how the money is allocated among different investment portfolios. While you may get higher returns on your retirement account with variable annuities, your return is not guaranteed.

With deferred annuities, the amounts you contribute during the **accumulation period** grow tax-deferred, and your earnings **compound**, meaning that your earnings have earnings of their own. After 20 years of tax-deferred growth at 8%, a $2,000 annual contribution could be worth $98,844—more than double the $40,000 you added.

To take advantage of that feature, you can buy what's called an **immediate annuity**. You make a single payment and the payout begins immediately, or at a time you choose within the first year.

Immediate fixed annuities provide the security of a guaranteed income. Even if returns on other investments slump—either because of falling interest rates, a weak economy, or shaky stock market—your annuity payments remain steady. And because you purchase the annuity outside of a qualified plan, a portion of the payments you receive will be a tax-free return of principal.

Immediate variable annuities also provide regular income, but the amount of each payment will vary to reflect the performance of the investment portfolios you have chosen.

Another alternative is to divide your immediate annuity into fixed and variable accounts, so that you'll have the assurance of a specific fixed income amount plus the opportunity to get increased income over time if your investment choices provide strong returns.

Immediate annuities appeal to people who receive a lump sum of money from a qualified retirement plan or from stock options, and who want to make sure that the money generates income for the rest of their lives. Immediate annuities may also be a smart solution for those who feel uncomfortable about managing an inheritance on their own.

2. Create a Personal Pension

MAKING COMPARISONS

In choosing nonqualified annuities, you should compare them to other types of investments, such as mutual funds. But in planning for retirement income, it also makes sense to compare annuities to employer pension plans.

How they resemble pensions

- Tax-deferred earnings
- Choice of ways to take income
- Option providing income stream for surviving spouse
- Income taxed at regular rates
- Death benefit to beneficiaries if you die before beginning to collect

How they differ from pensions

- Purchase made with after-tax dollars, so part of income payments may not be subject to tax
- Choice on when to begin withdrawals
- No limits on annuity purchase amounts, as there are with defined contribution pensions
- No limits on annuity income amounts

ISSUES OF AGE

Like all retirement plans that provide tax-deferred earnings, annuities have limits on withdrawals. If you withdraw before age 59½, you'll face a 10% penalty in addition to taxes due on the taxable earnings you withdraw. That's a condition the government imposes to discourage people from depleting their retirement resources and to ensure you have sufficient investments available when you retire. While there are some exceptions to the penalty rule, it's smart to consider annuities as a long-term commitment.

On the other hand, annuities can give you considerable flexibility in timing your withdrawals. Most pensions begin paying out your benefit when you retire, and you must begin withdrawals from an IRA by age 70½. With most nonqualified annuities, you can defer taking income until age 85 or later. That lets you pick the time when you want to start—perhaps when you'll be paying taxes at a lower rate.

Taxable Investing

A portfolio you manage yourself is another way to invest for retirement.

While having to juggle various sources of retirement income can be intimidating, there's a bright side. The bigger your overall investment portfolio, the more comfortable your retirement is likely to be.

That's why you don't want to lose sight of the role that investing on your own can play in providing long-term financial security. In addition to the money you put into employer-provided plans and tax-deferred retirement accounts, there are many other ways to invest for a comfortable retirement.

Investments you manage yourself, or with the help of a financial advisor, have a major advantage, provided you're willing to accept the responsibility: You can invest any amount you choose in any way you choose, and you can sell your investments any time you want. You can also give your assets away.

But investing this way does have a drawback. If your investments produce income, you'll owe tax on all that income at whatever your current tax rate is. That means up to 38.6% of what you earn in 2002 and 2003 goes into Uncle Sam's pockets—plus whatever percentage your state tax department collects. That top federal rate will drop gradually, however, to 37.6% for 2004 and 2005, and to 35% in 2006.

GROWTH, NOT INCOME

If you concentrate on producing income before you retire rather than investing for growth, you may find you're paying a lot in taxes and not increasing your net worth. While one rule of thumb suggests that the percentage of fixed-income investments in your portfolio should equal your age, most experts suggest that keeping 60% or more of your holdings in equities until you actually retire makes more sense.

INVESTING FOR GROWTH

When you're building a long-term portfolio, you want to consider investments that grow in value but don't produce current income. Even if you'll eventually use your investments to provide retirement income, you want to minimize the tax you'll owe as your investments grow.

- Mutual funds that stress long-term growth and follow a strategy of limited buying and selling of fund holdings (known as a **turnover rate**)
- Stocks that emphasize growth rather than paying dividends
- Index funds
- Nonqualified deferred annuities
- Real estate, including your home, which can be a long-term investment but can be more difficult to convert to cash

BUY

KNOWING WHAT YOU WANT

Long-term investments are centered on **return**, or growth of your assets, rather than **yield**, or how much they pay on an annual, quarterly or monthly basis. For example, an 8% annual **return** on a $10,000 growth investment would bump its value to $46,610 in 20 years if the annual increase remained in the account and compounded. But an 8% **yield** on a $10,000 fixed-income investment with the income taken out each year would pay you $16,000 over 20 years, plus the return of your $10,000, for a total of $26,000.

RICH ON PAPER

The wonderful thing about investing for growth is that you can increase the value of your stock portfolio and not owe a dime in taxes. As long as you hold onto an investment, all you have are **paper profits**. You see the gains on your statement, but they're unrealized. The only way to lock in the gains is to sell—and pay the tax you owe.

Of course there's no guarantee that your investment will maintain its paper value either. It's as easy to have paper losses, especially in the short run, as it is to have paper gains until the gains are realized.

CREATING AN INCOME STREAM

In order to turn equity investments, and stocks in particular, into retirement income, you may decide to sell off part of your holdings and put the lump sum after taxes into income-producing bonds or annuities.

Or you may work out a plan to tap a percentage of those holdings every year. If you own mutual funds, for example, you can withdraw the annual earnings and leave your principal intact. Or you can withdraw at a faster rate if you need more income, though in that case you're reducing the principal.

There are two potential problems with setting up a withdrawal plan:

- You can't predict what the rate of return, or earnings, will be from year to year, so you can't predict the income you can count on.
- You may have trouble determining which investments to sell and which to keep.

CAPITAL GAINS TAX

You do catch a tax break when you sell investments you've made a profit on. That increase in value is known as a capital gain, and long-term **capital gains** are taxed at a lower rate than ordinary income. To qualify for the rate, though, you have to own the investment more than a year.

If your regular tax rate is	Your long-term capital gains tax rate is
38.6%	20%
35%	20%
30%	20%
27%	20%
15%	10%

There are greater long-term capital gains savings in store for investments you hold at least five years before selling. If your regular rate is higher than 15%, the tax rate will be reduced from 20% to 18% for gains on investments you bought in 2001 and later. If you're in the 15% bracket, the rate will be reduced from 10% for 8% regardless of when you bought the investment.

With mutual funds, you pay capital gains tax each year if the fund has made a profit by selling investments it owned. But that income may not qualify for the long-term rate, as funds may buy and sell holdings within a one-year period.

HOLD **SELL**

Earnings reinvested	Paid annually (no reinvestment)
$10,000 growth investment with 8% annual return	$10,000 fixed income investment with 8% yield
after 20 years	
$46,610	$26,000

The $20,610 difference would actually be greater because you would pay tax on the fixed income each year, but could postpone taxes on any growth in value by holding onto the investment.

BUILDING YOUR ESTATE

One of the greatest benefits of building your own investment portfolio is that you can give your assets to your heirs while you're alive or leave them after your death. Unsold stock, for example, can be handed over to your heirs without your having to pay tax on any increase in value. And if you leave stock to someone in your will, that person inherits the stock at its current value and could sell it immediately without owing capital gains tax, or hold it as long as he or she wished. However, keep in mind that your estate might owe tax on the total value of your property.

Working for Extra Income

Just because you're retired doesn't mean you're not working.

Although the traditional retirement age is 65, many people retire earlier—the average typical age in 2001 was closer to 62. And many other people go on working into their 70s or longer. In some cases, you can collect a pension from one job while working full-time at another. Or you can work part-time for the same company from which you've retired. Check first, though. Sometimes there are restrictions on what's known as double-dipping, or collecting a salary and a pension from the same employer.

Good news: Income caps apply only to earned income.

LIMITS ON WORKING

You can work and collect Social Security at the same time, but there are limits on the amount you can earn between 62 and the month you turn 65 without losing some or all of your annual benefits. Those amounts, which are adjusted every year, are age-based, so that the year you turn 65 you can earn more without losing Social Security income.

You can also earn more than the cap in the year you retire, and still qualify for benefits. But there's a limit on what you can earn each month after your actual retirement date. For 2002, it is $940.

If you are	You can earn up to	After which you'll lose
62–64	**$11,280** in 2002	$1 for every $2 you earn over limit
turning 65	**$30,000** in 2002	$1 for every $3 you earn over limit
65+	**No limit**	**No penalty**

DEALING WITH SOCIAL SECURITY

If you're working and collecting benefits, you must estimate your earnings for the Social Security Administration (SSA), using a form called an Annual Report of Earnings. If you expect to earn more than the limit for any year, the SSA reduces the number of checks you receive, based on your estimate.

If it turns out that you earn less than you estimated, then the SSA will issue a check to make up what you're owed. If you earn more than you estimated, you'll have to repay the SSA the excess benefits, either in installments or a lump sum. In either case, you submit form SSA-777 and a copy of your tax form to the SSA to verify your earnings.

Trying to keep the SSA in the dark is a bad idea. If you don't report that you're working, you'll have to pay a penalty as well as return any overpayment of benefits you do receive.

STARTING AGAIN

You can change your mind about the right time to begin collecting Social Security, or can suspend your benefits after you've started collecting. That means whether you want to go back to work or feel you have to, you won't get bogged down with paperwork trying to estimate your potential earnings.

For example, if you retire at 62 and go back to work at 63, you can end your benefits, repay what you've received, and postpone collecting until the next time you retire. Since you'll be contributing again, you're likely to increase the base amount on which the new benefit is figured.

SPENDING VERSUS INVESTING

One of the major decisions you'll face if you work after you retire is how to use your earnings. When you can invest these earnings in a retirement program, such as an IRA, an annuity or a salary reduction plan, it may be best to live on unearned or investment income, including your pension. That allows your post-retirement earnings to grow tax-deferred so you'll have more assets to convert to income in the future.

When you do stop working for good, or if you need the money in an emergency and are older than 59½, you have the added advantage of being able to withdraw the money for any purpose without owing a penalty.

According to Social Security

If you work less than 15 hours a MONTH you're RETIRED	If you work more than 45 hours a MONTH you're NOT RETIRED

WORKING PART TIME

You may be thinking about working after retirement because you need more money to live on, or because you'd like extra cash to spend on things you enjoy. Working part-time could mean you'd continue to be eligible for your full Social Security benefits.

For example, if you were between ages 62 and 64 and earned $200 a week, you'd still be eligible for your full Social Security benefit. But the extra $800 a month could make the difference between feeling secure and being forced to cut back on necessities, or between being able to take a cross-country trip and having to stay home.

Many employers like part-time workers because they don't have to provide health insurance, retirement plans, and other benefits. If you've got retirement health benefits, for example, or qualify for Medicare, you don't need coverage at your post-retirement job. You may also find part-time positions that are open to people who can work during school hours, when young people are in class.

WHEN IT ISN'T WORK

Though there are limits on what you can earn before you begin to lose Social Security income, there are no limits on how busy you can be. Many charitable, cultural, and social service organizations depend on volunteers to make their programs run, and are always looking for people who have time to help out. As a little bonus, you may be able to take a tax deduction for your transportation expenses.

Taxes

Income taxes, like weeds, can be hard to get under control.

Despite the major changes that retirement is likely to bring, you won't be able to escape taxes entirely if you have income from a job, a pension, investments or Social Security. The irony, of course, is that if you owe no tax, you're likely to be in really serious financial trouble.

There are some tax breaks, though, after retirement. When you stop working, you stop paying taxes for Social Security and Medicare. That can add several thousand dollars to your bottom line. If you earn a pension in one state but move to another, you don't have to pay taxes on the pension income to the state where you earned it. (But you will be a taxpayer in the state where you live.) When you reach 65, you may also qualify for a larger standard deduction when you file your federal tax return.

TAXING RULES

Most retirement income is taxed, based on the type of income it is. Here's an overview of rules that apply nationwide.

Annuity income: A portion of each annuity payment is considered a return of principal and is not taxed unless it was purchased with pretax dollars. Earnings are taxed at your regular rate.

Capital gains: Profits from the sale of stock, mutual funds, real estate, and other equity investments are taxed at your capital gains rate, provided you have held the investments for the required period.

Dividends on stock, dividend and interest **distributions** from mutual funds, and **interest** on taxable bonds, CDs, and savings accounts are taxed at your regular rate.

IRA distributions: All earnings in a traditional IRA and any contribution for which you took a tax deduction are taxed at your regular rate when you withdraw the money. Withdrawals of nondeductible investments you made are not subject to tax.

Lump sum distributions from annuities, pensions, 401(k)s, and other salary-reduction plans are taxed at your regular rate. If you were born before 1936, you may be eligible for income averaging, which lets you spread the taxation over a ten-year period and may reduce the total you owe.

Pension annuity income is taxed at your regular rate.

Rollovers from pensions, 401(k)s, and other salary reduction plans remain tax-deferred until you make withdrawals.

Income tax on part of annuity income

Capital gains tax

Tax on interest and dividends

Income tax on IRA withdrawals

10% penalty on early withdrawals

Tax on lump sum distribution

TAX TRIMMER

BRACKETS AND RATES

The amount of tax you owe on your regular income depends on two factors, the rates at which various levels and types of income are taxed and the tax bracket you're in.

A **tax rate** is the percentage of tax paid on a certain level of income. For 2002 and following, there are six rates in the U.S., and you pay the lowest rate on a base amount of income and then at increasingly higher rates each time your income passes another cut-off, or level. Those levels, or plateaus of income, are set each year to reflect inflation.

For example, if your taxable income was high enough in 2002 to cross three brackets, you'd pay tax at the 10% rate on income in the lowest bracket, at the 15% rate on income in the next bracket, and at the 27% rate on the rest.

within five years. But if you don't repay, you'll face the 10% penalty as well as the taxes due.

There's a 50% penalty due each year on any amount you should withdraw from your traditional IRA but fail to take after you reach age 70½. There's also a 6% annual penalty for excess IRA contributions in your account even if your spouse or employer added the extra amount. Any contributions in the year you turn 70½ are also considered excess contributions and incur the penalty.

You might also owe a penalty if you withdraw a lump sum from a qualified plan. The plan will withhold 20% of the total toward your tax bill. If you roll over the money into an IRA, you can reclaim the amount when you file your income tax return for the year. The problem is that you must put the total amount—including the 20% you didn't

INCOME TAX RATES ARE BEING REDUCED

The four top federal income tax rates will drop gradually through tax year 2006.

Calendar Year	28% rate reduced to:	31% rate reduced to:	36% rate reduced to:	39.6% rate reduced to:
2001[1]–2003	27%	30%	35%	38.6%
2004–2005	26%	29%	34%	37.6%
2006 and later	25%	28%	33%	35%

[1] Effective July 1, 2001

Your **marginal tax rate** is the highest rate at which you pay tax on any of your taxable income. In the example above, you'd be in the 27% bracket for 2002 and 2003. Most people expect to be in a lower bracket after they retire because they expect their taxable income to be less.

EXTRA TAXES

You should be able to avoid taxes that are imposed as penalties, though it's your job to comply with the regulations.

Withdrawals from retirement plans before you reach age 59½ may be subject to a 10% penalty in addition to income tax you owe. You can withdraw certain amounts from IRAs without penalty to pay medical and higher education bills and up to $10,000 to buy a first home.

You can borrow from some retirement plans without penalty, as long as you pay the amount back

Tax on pension annuity income

get—into the IRA. If you don't deposit it all, even if it's because you don't have the money, the 20% is considered a withdrawal, so tax is due on the amount, and potentially the 10% early withdrawal penalty. You can avoid the problem by doing a direct rollover.

SOME INCOME IS TAX FREE

Just as you can minimize the tax you owe by choosing the way you take income, you can avoid tax altogether by making tax-exempt investments.

You owe no federal tax on interest you earn on municipal bonds sold by state and local governments (and no state tax if you live in the state where the bond is issued). There's no state or local tax on interest you earn on U.S. Treasury bonds, notes, and bills.

And if you wait to take money from a Roth IRA until you're older than 59½ and the account has been open at least five years, you'll owe no income tax on the amount you withdraw.

While you probably won't be able to produce all the income you need from these sources—there are limits on what you can contribute to a tax-exempt Roth IRA and interest income is vulnerable to inflation—they can leave you with more income by eliminating taxes.

Creating Income

Your first job is putting together the income you'll need to live comfortably.

Remember the retirement rule of thumb: You'll need roughly 80% of your preretirement income to live the way you've grown accustomed to. To provide that successfully, you'll need to get your finances in order.

BEFORE

Building Your Mental Accounts

You don't walk into a bank or brokerage firm to open a mental account. It's a way of organizing your assets in your mind, separating the money for living expenses from what you're using to build your investment portfolio.

If you've spent much of your investing life protecting your principal and increasing your net worth, it may be a jolt to readjust your thinking to start spending what you've worked hard to accumulate. One approach may be to divide your retirement assets themselves into three categories: one for income, one for emergencies (including long-term healthcare), and the third for continued growth.

Income. Some of your current investments, such as bonds, may already produce income on a monthly, quarterly or annual basis. Others, such as annuities, can be easily converted to an income stream. Others can be sold and the proceeds used to buy bonds or annuities.

Emergencies. It's important to have investments that you can count on if you have a medical or other emergency that isn't covered by insurance. Liquidity is important, so the assets can be readily converted to cash. So is stability. You don't want to worry about having to sell your investments at a loss because you're under pressure to get the cash. Investments you might consider to provide both liquidity and stability are U.S. Treasury bills, money market mutual funds, and CDs.

Growth. Part of your retirement account should be producing additional growth, to increase the probability that you'll have money available as long as you live. The same type of equity investments that worked to build your assets are likely to be smart choices for continued growth as well, though you may want to emphasize more dividend-paying stocks, equity income or growth and income mutual funds, or similar investment portfolios within a variable annuity.

THINKING IT THROUGH

- Calculating what you can expect from various sources
- Analyzing the tax implications of withdrawing from those sources
- Deciding the order in which to draw on your income sources, based in part on their growth potential
- Figuring out how to ensure you'll have enough money to live on for as long as you need it

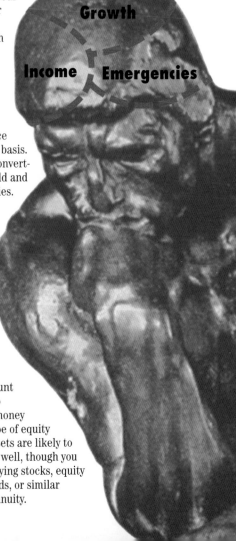

Growth

Income Emergencies

UNDERSTANDING GROWTH

One of the reasons for stressing growth potential in making long-term retirement plan choices is that the value of your investment accounts can increase even after you begin to take income. For example, the market price of a stock that is paying an annual 4% dividend may increase by twice that percentage, or 8%, in a year. That would mean a stock selling at $75 could increase in value to $81. Instead of receiving $3,000 in income on 1,000 shares, you'd get $3,240—more than enough to offset a 3% inflation rate—and you'd still own the stock. You could get similar, though not necessarily equal, gains in value if you owned variable annuities or mutual funds that owned a stock such as the one in this example.

Of course, in any given period a stock's price can also go down, as can the value of annuity accounts and mutual funds.

AFTER

Using Your Mental Accounts

Perhaps your primary challenge will be providing the additional annual income you'll need from various investment sources. And remember that keeping ahead of inflation means that the dollar amount you'll need in the first year after you retire is likely to increase each year.

SPEND IT OR SAVE IT?

When you're deciding which investments to convert to income and which ones to leave alone, here are some questions to ask yourself or your financial advisor:

- How will the income be taxed and how much will be left to spend?
- Will you get a lump sum or a series of regular payments?
- Do you face any penalties for converting the investment to income?
- What will your beneficiaries owe in tax if you leave them the investment rather than using it to provide retirement income?

THE INCOME IN PLACE

As you analyze the income you'll have in retirement, it's a good idea to start with the amount you'll need and the money you can count on. That will tell you how much you have to provide from your own investments.

If you were earning $78,000 when you retired, and had a defined contribution pension, you might find your situation looks something like the one shown in this example.

Preretirement income	**$78,000**
	x .80
Estimated income needs	= **$62,400**
Estimated Social Security	– **$16,000**
Estimated pension	– **$12,000**
Additional income needed	= **$34,400**

PUTTING TOGETHER THE REST

IRA income from $200,000 account	**$10,000**		IRA income from $300,000 account	**$14,000**
Income from variable annuity	**+ $15,000**		Income from variable annuity	**+ $12,000**
Distributions from stock mutual fund	**+ $ 7,000**	**OR**	$75,000 in stock yielding 4%	**+ $ 3,000**
Interest on bond paying 5.5%	**+ $ 5,500**		Interest on a bond paying 5.5%	**+ $ 5,500**
Investment income	= **$37,500**		Investment income	= **$34,500**

Though your own income resources may be different from the ones in these examples, you can get a sense of what's involved in anticipating the sources for your income stream.

Anticipating the Unexpected

You can't be sure what's going to happen next—but
you can be prepared.

No matter how carefully you prepare for retirement,
there's always something you can't predict. Sometimes
you're surprised by good news, such as a generous
inheritance or years of strong investment performance.
But it's important to be realistic in your planning. That
means taking precautionary steps to cushion yourself,
and those who are dependent on you, from the financial strains that can result from illness, unstable
economic markets, and other problems.

ILLNESS

Nobody plans on being sick, but the reality is that as
you grow older you are increasingly vulnerable to
illness or injury. So it pays to plan ahead. First, you
need good health insurance. But you also need a
steady source of income that you can activate
when you need it, and can count on to last your
lifetime—even if you live to be 100 plus.

You can use different types of insurance to
help protect your financial health.

SOCIAL

SECURITY

LONG-TERM

CARE

DISABILITY

INSURANCE

PENSION

FUND

ANNUITY

INCOME

ANTICIPATING
THE PREDICTABLE

Among the eventualities you have to
anticipate is the possibility of dying
while others are dependent on you
for financial support. One of the
ways to help protect them is to have
adequate life insurance. Similarly,
you might leave an estate large
enough to generate a substantial
estate-tax bill, which the death
benefit paid on a life insurance trust
could meet. That's why most experts
agree that life insurance plays an
essential part in your long-term
financial planning.

IN YOUR COURT

While you're increasingly responsible for providing for your long-term needs, the opportunities you have to meet the challenge are expanding as well. There are more investments available: more varieties of annuities, more mutual funds, more ways to buy stocks. There are more employer sponsored plans, with more choices in the plans. And there's growing flexibility in the ways you can turn your assets into income.

You can begin by analyzing your current financial situation, to assess the income you know you can count on after you retire.

The next step is building an investment portfolio that will provide the other income you'll need. That involves deciding which of the investment categories you're comfortable using. Among the factors to consider are your tolerance for risk, your commitment to growth, and how confident you feel about making financial decisions.

Then you'll want to create a plan for allocating money to the investments you've chosen and begin building and strengthening your portfolio.

Long-term care insurance is designed to cover custodial healthcare over an extended period of time. Keep in mind, if you are considering this approach, that the premiums and cost of the insurance will be greater the later you buy. If you try to purchase a long-term policy in your 70s, for example, the premiums may be prohibitive. But if you buy earlier, and cheaper, the benefits your plan offers may be vulnerable to inflation since the reimbursement amounts are often fixed. You should look for a plan that automatically boosts the benefits as time goes by or lets you buy additional coverage to offset inflation.

Disability insurance pays you a percentage of your salary if you can't work, and **catastrophic illness insurance** covers your medical costs if you exceed the upper limit your regular health insurer will pay.

An alternative to insurance is to buy a variable annuity to provide income you can use to cover the costs of long-term care or disability should the need arise. Or you could arrange to use the annuity benefit to actually pay the premium for a long-term care policy.

DROP IN INVESTMENT VALUE

Another reality you have to face is that your investments can lose value, at least in the short term. Or interest rates can drop and reduce your anticipated income.

When equity markets produce strong earnings, it's easy to forget that prices and dividends can move down as well as up. So while you need equity investments for long-term growth, counting on their performance on a daily basis can be unsettling. For example, if you're planning on an 11% annual return on your mutual fund investments, so that you can withdraw at that rate and not eat into your principal, a period of lower returns can disrupt your plans.

The same is true of fixed-income investments. If you have money invested in older bonds paying at 7.5% and the best rate you can find to reinvest your principal is 5.5% when a bond matures, your annual income on a $100,000 bond investment would drop $2,000, or 26.6%.

CHANGING TAX RULES

Over time, tax laws are modified to reflect changes in the economy, shifts in political thinking, and evolving attitudes toward investing. For example, the penalty for excess withdrawals from IRAs and other retirement plans has been dropped and the ceiling on contributions to other plans has been raised.

Of course, there's no way to predict the rate at which you may have to pay taxes on your future earnings, or whether the rules governing tax-deferred investing will be tightened. There have been big changes in both areas in recent years. But in the meantime, you can take advantage of the existing opportunities to build your retirement assets and hope for the best.

What sometimes happens, though, is that existing rules are **grandfathered**. That means they continue to apply to existing plans, but not to new ones.

Investment Basics

Investing can make the difference between hoping you can afford to retire and knowing you can.

Whether you plan to retire in three or thirty years, taking personal responsibility for providing the financial security you'll need to live comfortably isn't just smart—it's a necessity. That means figuring out how you can create a dependable stream of income that will run as long as you need it, as well as income to use for special things you plan to do or buy in retirement. The key is **investing**, or putting the money you already have to work so that it's producing the money you need.

SAVING VERSUS INVESTING

Making the leap from saving to investing is crucial to making sure you're financially prepared for retirement. **Saving** means socking money away, typically in a bank savings or mutual fund money market account, where you earn a relatively low rate of interest. **Investing**, by contrast, means owning assets, such as stocks or real estate, which over time produce far more substantial earnings than a savings account. You can also invest in a bond by lending money to a company or the government in exchange for the guarantee of regular income and eventual return of the loan amount.

COMPOUNDING

Compounding is one of the key ways your money makes more money. Here's how it works: When you invest $100 in an account that earns 10% each year, you'll have $110 at the end of the first year. At the end of the second year, you'll have $121 in your account. That $1 is the **compound earnings**, or earnings earned on earnings. Compounding becomes particularly profitable when your investment grows undisturbed over many years and you add money to the account regularly. If you invest $2,000 a year in an account for 20 years, your investment will total $40,000. If the investment is earning 8% annually, you'll have amassed $98,844.

STICK WITH IT

Investments grow best when they are nurtured with regular infusions of new money. That way, you're building the base on which you're earning.

$2,000 invested yearly, earning 8%	Can add up to
10 years	$ 31,291
20 years	$ 98,844
30 years	$244,692

TIME IS YOUR FRIEND

If you need your investment assets to make a down payment or for some other short-term use, your primary goal is to be sure your principal is safe. Investing for retirement, however, demands a different way of thinking. You should keep these three goals in mind:

- **Making your assets grow**. When you invest you want your principal, or money you have accumulated, to grow and increase in value so it can earn more money in the future
- **Producing income from your investments**. After you retire, you'll need investment money to supplement your income from pensions and Social Security
- **Preserving some of your principal while spending down the rest**. You'll want to strike a balance between maintaining steady growth and making sure you have enough to live on

OR TAX DEFERRAL

...hich you can convert an invest-
...called its **liquidity**. Money in
a bank savings account is obviously very liquid
because you can take out the money at any time.
Similarly, stocks are sometimes considered liquid
investments because they can be sold fairly easily.
The difference is that with stocks and other equities, there is the risk of losing money if you have
to sell when the market is down. In either
case, one downside of liquidity is that
the money you earn in savings or
from stock dividends or
sales is taxable
each year.

By contrast, investments in certain retirement
plans such as 401(k)s, TSAs, IRAs and annuities
have the benefit of tax-deferred growth. That
means you owe no taxes on earnings until you
begin to withdraw. As a not-so-subtle encourage-
ment to hold these investments until retirement,
in most cases you'll owe a 10% penalty tax to
the federal government on taxable withdrawals
before you reach 59½. That makes the
accounts **illiquid**, or less convertible
to cash. By sacrificing some degree
of liquidity in these accounts,
though, you benefit from
compounding as well
as tax-deferral.

INVEST EARLY AND OFTEN

Ultimately, investing for retirement takes
a combination of time and money. The
more time you have between now and
retirement, the less you will have to
put away each year and the greater
opportunity you will have to grow
your money. For example,
suppose you had $10,000 in
an IRA at age 35, and made no
more contributions. If the account
grew at 8% a year for 30 years—
until you retired at age 65—it would
be worth $100,630. That's because tax-
deferred, compound interest has enough
time to work its magic. On the other hand,
if you were 45 before you had $10,000 in
your IRA, and it grew at 8% a year for 20
years, it would be worth only $46,610.

Ideally, though, you continue to
contribute throughout your life. If you
put just $2,000 into a tax-deferred plan
each year for 30 years, it would add up to
$244,692 if the earnings accumulated at
8% a year.

And it's never too late to start, even
though it's true that the longer you wait
the more you'd have to commit to build a
large accumulation by age 65. Since you're
likely to live 20, 30 or more years after 65,
the investments you make in your 40s or
50s also have a long growth period and
can make a big difference to your sense
of financial security.

SEEKING GROWTH

Growth, or increase in
the size and value of your accounts, is the basic principle of
retirement investing. There are a
number of ways to achieve growth. One
way is to set aside a regular amount in your
investments, such as adding 15% of your
earnings every paycheck. Another way
is to reinvest the earnings from your
investments, rather than spending
them. Finally, you can achieve
growth by concentrating on
investments that characteris-
tically increase in value
including stocks, mutual
funds, and the invest-
ment portfolios of
variable annuities
that offer stock
investments.

Investment Markets

If you want to buy an investment, you shop where it's for sale.

Investment professionals use the term **market** to describe the physical places where investments are bought and sold and also the activity of buying and selling. U.S. markets have come a long way from the time traders met under a buttonwood tree in lower Manhattan. For example, trading is increasingly handled electronically, at a split-second pace, and the number of daily transactions has skyrocketed. At the same time investors have more and more choices, both in types of investments and ways to buy them.

THE MAJOR MARKETS

The ups and downs of Wall Street that dominate investment news describe the activity of the U.S. **stock market**. There are two major stock markets—the New York Stock Exchange, commonly known as the NYSE, and the Nasdaq, a sophisticated **electronic stock market** run by the National Association of Securities Dealers. Through those markets you can buy shares of stock issued by thousands of different companies. In fact, millions of shares change hands every day on the NYSE and Nasdaq, and on smaller markets across the country. Millions more are traded on markets around the world.

The **bond market** refers to the trading of corporate, government, and agency bonds with different maturities or yields. There are really two bond markets, the exchange market and the over-the-counter (OTC) market. You can also buy bonds when they are issued by corporations, local governments, and government agencies. Using a system known as Treasury Direct, you can buy Treasury bills and notes directly from the U.S. Treasury.

The **mutual fund market** isn't a single place, and neither is the **real estate market**, but active buying and selling goes on constantly in those investments. One major way they differ from the stock and bond markets is that it's possible for you to buy and sell on your own.

Investing lets you tap into the energy of the markets.

INVESTMENT VOCABULARY

Here are some terms to help you build an investment vocabulary.

Securities refer to investments like stocks and bonds. The term originally described the pieces of paper, like stock certificates, that represented ownership.

Publicly held describes a company whose stock is owned by outside investors. A private company goes public by issuing stock to such investors.

Secondary market refers to securities that are bought and sold following their original issue. A stock exchange is a secondary market.

Using a Broker

To buy or sell stocks and bonds, you open an account with a **brokerage house**, or investment firm. Stockbrokers working for those firms take orders and either relay them to the floor of an exchange, enter them in an exchange's computerized matching system, or trade them on Nasdaq's electronic stock market.

Some brokerage houses, known as **full service brokers**, offer their clients a range of services, including advice about their portfolios, recommendations about trades, in-house research departments, and sometimes full scale financial planning. **Discount brokers**, by contrast, simply buy and sell stock at your instruction, without offering advice. As the names suggest, the commissions, or sales charges for handling your trades, are typically significantly higher for full service brokers than for discount or deep discount brokers.

Increasingly, too, you can do your securities trading online, by opening an electronic account with a brokerage firm on the World Wide Web. There are lots of advantages to trading electronically, including speed, convenience, and generally lower fees than conventional investing.

Buying Mutual Funds

When you buy mutual funds, you're a step removed from the process of investing in stocks and bonds. Rather than choosing the individual investments on your own, you choose a mutual fund that typically invests in one or the other, or sometimes in both.

You can buy mutual funds either directly from mutual fund companies or through a financial advisor, brokerage house, or bank. Mutual fund companies typically offer a variety of funds, known as a **fund family**, to choose among. Each fund within the family makes different kinds of investments, and you can select just one or several different funds. Many fund families allow you to switch assets between different funds within the family—a process known as **exchanging** funds—at little to no cost (though it is likely you will owe income taxes on any gain in the fund you're selling).

Or, you can choose to invest in a variety of different fund families rather than buying several funds in one family. Sometimes a certain family has stronger funds in one category than another, and you can mix and match to put together the strongest collection of funds.

Simplified Shopping

If you haven't built a relationship with a brokerage house and aren't ready to try online investing, you can do your investment shopping closer to home.

Many **banks** now offer a variety of investment products, such as annuities, mutual funds, and securities. Some mutual fund companies offer funds from many fund families in addition to the ones they sponsor themselves. These **mutual fund supermarkets** make investing easier, since it's one-stop shopping. What's more, you get a single statement covering all of your funds, simplifying your recordkeeping.

You can also find investment information through an **insurance company**. They offer overall financial planning and access to investments including annuities and mutual funds.

Many **financial planners**, who work either in private practices or with national planning companies, offer help with retirement planning, from tax preparation to investment advice. Many of them also sell annuities and other securities.

Risk And Return

When you invest wisely, you weigh risks and returns.

Risk is the chance you take of losing money on an investment. The extent of your **risk** is directly related to your potential **return**, or the amount you can make. The relationship is fairly simple: the greater the risk, the greater the opportunity for substantial return.

Investments such as money market funds, CDs, Treasury bonds, or fixed annuities expose you to little or no risk to principal. In most cases, they pay you what they promise to pay, based on a particular rate of interest. The trade-off is that these investments offer limited return because they don't grow in value as much as other investments. High-risk securities like stock in start-up companies or derivative products, such as options and futures, offer potentially high return but at the very real risk of losing your investment capital. Between these extremes are a large number of

Return is the amount you earn on your investment

investments that let you weigh moderate risk against the potential for substantial return. Among other things, the list includes stocks, stock mutual funds, and variable annuities.

Risk is the chance you take of losing money on an investment

EVALUATING RISK

Investment professionals use several formulas for evaluating risk that you can read about in the financial press or ask your advisor to explain when you are weighing different investments. A typical one measures a stock's **risk ratio**, or how much the investment might increase in value versus how much it might fall.

For example, a stock with a share price of $50 that analysts predict could go to $80 (a $30 gain), but could potentially fall to $40 (a $10 loss), has a risk ratio of 3:1, or $30 up/$10 down. Similarly, if the stock might rise only $5 but could fall $25, its risk ratio is 1:5, and it's a much more risky investment.

INVESTMENT A
A Good Risk Ratio

3
TO
1

Possible rise in price

Possible drop in price

INVESTMENT B
A Bad Risk Ratio

1
TO

5

MEASURING RISK

One measure of risk is an investment's **volatility**, or how much its value can change within a short period of time. Another measure is **predictability** of performance. A low-risk investment is predictable and not volatile, while exactly the opposite is true of a high-risk one.

One of the big factors in assessing risk is your investment time frame. If you want your investments to produce predictable returns and you plan to use them in the short term, you can afford less risk. But the longer you have, the more risk you can afford to take since any short-term decline in value can be offset over time.

Investing wisely is a little more complicated than choosing minimal risk for short-term goals and higher risk for long-term ones.

When you invest for retirement, you probably do not want to put all of your money into higher risk securities, for fear of losing the assets you'll need when you retire. And from the short-term perspective, the less time you have before you plan to retire, the more risk you may need to accept to reach your goals.

THE BIGGEST RISKS

The biggest risk you can take with your financial future is to delay. And most experts agree that the second most serious is not investing for growth.

THREE BASIC RISK MODELS

Investors tend to fall into three categories, and make their decisions accordingly.

Conservative

These investors are willing to sacrifice return for limited risk, concentrating on investments with a fixed rate of return, including liquid investments such as money market funds, U.S. Treasury bills, CDs and fixed annuities.

Moderate

These investors will take some risk to get higher return. Their portfolios might include a mix of growth stocks and bonds, as well as mutual funds and variable annuities that invest in stocks and bonds.

Aggressive

These investors are willing to speculate, investing some of their portfolio in securities with unpredictable results. Those investments might include speculative stocks and mutual funds, derivatives, high-yield bonds, and private (rather than publicly traded) investments.

OTHER TYPES OF RISK

In addition to volatility and predictability, there are other risks to consider when making your investments:

Market risk is the chance that the entire stock market or economy as a whole may stumble. In the event of an overall market decline, your stocks will probably drop in value, regardless of how the company is doing.

Business risk is the risk that if the performance of a business declines, the value of the stock will decline as well. Among the factors that influence business performance are how the company is managed, whether its products or services are in demand, and how much debt it has.

Inflation risk is the risk that the rising costs of goods and products will erode the value of an investment over time. This is particularly worrisome with fixed-income instruments like bonds, CDs or fixed annuities, where the interest rate is set for a period of time into the future.

Credit risk is the risk that a creditor will be unable to pay its debt. This is a risk consideration for investors in corporate bonds, for example, where you must look at a company's credit rating in order to assess its ability to repay its debt. The more risk of nonpayment you are willing to assume, the greater the interest rate the bonds often pay.

Currency risk is the risk that the value of an investment can and will fluctuate as the value of a particular country's currency, or relative value as compared to the U.S. dollar, changes. This is a factor if you are investing in international stocks, bonds, or mutual funds.

What's in a Guarantee?

There are few guarantees when you invest, but some investments provide more than others.

Because investing involves entrusting your money to someone or some organization—such as a bank, an insurance company, or a fund family—or to the management ability of a corporation whose stocks or bonds you buy, you take a certain amount of risk that you may lose some or all of your money. While that's the case with some investments, others are designed to provide security and ensure that your principal will not disappear.

IN THE NAME OF THE FED

Savings accounts, CDs, and bank money market accounts are popular investments, if only for one reason: They're safe. Even if the bank fails, its deposits are protected by the Federal Deposit Insurance Corporation (FDIC).

There are some limits. Each depositor is insured for up to $100,000 in each of five categories in each bank. The categories are individual, joint, retirement, trust, and business accounts.

For example, if you have $100,000 in an individual account and that much in an IRA, all of your money is safe. But if your IRA is worth $125,000, $25,000 of it would not be insured. On the other hand, if you had three separate IRA accounts in three separate banks, each worth $100,000, all of the money would be insured.

Two words of caution: Separate branches of the same bank aren't considered separate banks. If a bank is bought by another bank, deposits

THE TRADE OFFS

With guaranteed investments, you generally trade the expectation of a smaller return for the assurance of knowing your money is safe and your income will be regular.

Advantages

- There's little chance of losing your principal

- With a guaranteed investment, like a fixed immediate annuity, you generally receive a fixed rate of return, so you will always know how much income to expect

  - Despite ups and downs in the financial markets or the economy as a whole, guaranteed investments continue to pay what they promise

  - In most cases when you make a guaranteed investment, there are no additional decisions to make until it matures

Disadvantages

- Guaranteed investments typically offer lower returns over the long term than other investments

- With a fixed rate of return, you run the risk that inflation could outpace your return and cause you to lose purchasing power

- Some guaranteed investments are less liquid than those without protection against loss of principal, or charge penalty fees if you liquidate early

continue to be insured, though the rates the purchasing bank pays on your accounts may change. That's because banks that acquire or merge with other banks are under no obligation to pay the same rates on any investment vehicle your old bank offered.

Equally important, the insurance applies only to money that's actually deposited in bank accounts. Mutual funds and annuities, for example, aren't covered by FDIC insurance, even if they carry the bank's name.

YEAR IN AND YEAR OUT

Certain annuities also offer guarantees. When you buy a fixed immediate annuity, for example, you immediately begin receiving a regular retirement income for the period of time you choose. The guarantee of a payment and its amount are written in the contract you sign with the insurance company.

If you choose a variable immediate annuity, the amount of your payment will fluctuate with the performance of the investments in the portfolios you have chosen. But you do have a guarantee that the payment will arrive on schedule.

Similarly, a fixed deferred annuity earns at least its guaranteed minimum rate of return, called the floor, and may earn more if the current interest rate is higher than the floor.

THEIR WORD IS THEIR BOND

Certain bonds are guaranteed as well. The principal of U.S. Treasury bonds, notes and bills is guaranteed by the borrower, the U.S. government. Similarly, U.S. savings bonds, which can be bought through banks, can be redeemed at face value at maturity. Government agency

bonds aren't guaranteed by the Treasury, but they're considered almost as good as Treasurys because of their connection with the government.

Insured corporate bonds are known as **pre-refunded bonds**. They're usually highly rated to begin with, and their repayment is guaranteed by money invested in U.S. Treasurys. Like all guaranteed investments, they pay a lower rate of interest than comparable nonguaranteed bonds.

THE INFLATION ISSUE

The U.S. Treasury issues inflation-indexed bonds, which guarantee principal but adjust the interest rates they pay to keep pace with inflation. The bond yields are linked to some measures of inflation so their value remains relatively constant.

In periods of high inflation, investors benefit because their buying power isn't undercut by increasing prices. But when inflation is low, the government makes out better because it can pay a lower rate of interest on a guaranteed long-term bond than on one that isn't indexed for inflation.

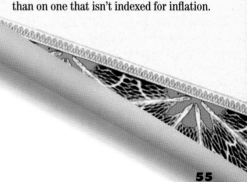

The **Securities Investor Protection Corporation (SIPC)** protects its members' securities customers for claims up to $500,000 (including $100,000 for claims in cash). SIPC protects against brokerage firm failure, however, not against the risk that your investments could lose value.

Spreading Your Assets Around

Diversification and asset allocation are the keys to a balanced portfolio.

It's an old saying that's worth repeating: You don't want all your eggs in one basket. The same rule applies to investing. If you put all your investments in one place, then your financial security rests on the strength of that single investment.

In order to diffuse risk, you need to **diversify**, or spread your assets among a variety of investments. The more diversified you are, the less likely that your portfolio as a whole will suffer if one or two securities perform poorly. In effect, diversification is like shock absorbers on a car, helping you glide over the bumps in the road.

NO SCATTER SHOTS

Diversification doesn't mean making random investments or simply accumulating a lot of investments for the sake of owning them. In fact, it's just the opposite. Diversification is about finding the right mix of investments to match your goals, given your age, the amount you have to invest, and your risk tolerance.

INSTANT DIVERSITY

Mutual funds offer instant diversity and a way to expand an already diversified portfolio with holdings that can be difficult to

THE BIG PICTURE
Creating a diversified portfolio is a process.

 1 **Create a plan for accumulating the money you'll use to invest.** Set up an investment account you can build with periodic deposits, identify investments you can add to regularly, even in small amounts, and earmark at least a portion of all gifts, bonuses or other windfalls for investing.

 2 **Define your goals.** To identify the right mix of investments for your portfolio, you have to know what you want to achieve and how much time you have to reach your goal. The more directly you can link a goal with an investment strategy, the better direction you have.

 3 **Match categories of investments to specific goals.** If you are investing long-term for retirement, you should consider equity investments, including stocks, stock mutual funds, and variable annuities. If you're recently retired, you might buy fixed income investments, like corporate or municipal bonds or fixed annuities to provide balance for your stock investments.

 4 **Choose specific investments within each category.** Finding the right stock, bond, mutual fund or annuity depends on understanding how quality performance is measured. You can get help from your investment advisor and learn as much as you can from what you read or listen to on the subject.

DIVERSITY WITHIN
A diversified portfolio typically has a mix of stocks, bonds, and cash, including the mutual funds that invest in them. You can and should also diversify within each of those specific categories of investments, called **asset classes**.

In other words, within the universe of stocks, there are a variety of companies, of different sizes and with different businesses. But if all the stocks you own are in technology companies, the equity side of your portfolio is not very diversified. To get greater balance, you could add stock in financial, manufacturing, and utility companies, for example.

If all your income investments are short term, such as CDs or Treasury bills, you might want to balance them with long-term bonds. Similarly, investments in non-U.S. assets are a good way of adding further diversification to your portfolio because they don't necessarily respond to the same economic factors as domestic companies.

amass on your own, including international stocks or Ginnie Mae bonds.

Funds offer the benefit of diversification within an asset class or sometimes across classes. Typically, an equity fund owns shares in 60 to 100 or more companies across a range of products and services. A balanced fund might own 60% equities and 40% bonds, the classic allocation of a professional retirement portfolio.

One caution is worth heeding, though. If you build a portfolio with three different large-company growth funds, you're not as diversified as you would be with one large-company fund, one small-company fund, and a fund focused on buying shares in undervalued or out-of-favor companies.

ASSET ALLOCATION

Once you decide on the asset classes to invest in, you have to decide how much of your investment dollars will go into each investment type. In other words, you have to create a model of how you will divide your investments. This is known as **asset allocation**.

Allocation models differ depending on your risk tolerance, time frame, and goals. Generally, the younger you are, the more heavily weighted toward equities your portfolio should be, since you're seeking long-term growth. A fairly aggressive investor in her 30s, for example, might have 90% of her portfolio in stocks, while a moderate investor in his 60s might have 60% of his portfolio in fixed income investments.

Since some growth is important in all portfolios, even the most conservative investors and those well into retirement are wise to allocate at least a small percentage of their assets to equities.

Many experts argue that asset allocation rather than the individual investments you own accounts for 90% or more of the results you get as an investor. To help you find the model that meets your needs, many companies and financial planners have computer programs to help you personalize a model.

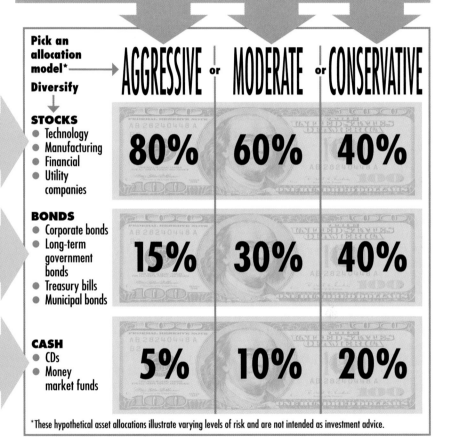

Pick an allocation model*

Diversify

AGGRESSIVE or **MODERATE** or **CONSERVATIVE**

STOCKS
- Technology
- Manufacturing
- Financial
- Utility companies

80%   **60%**   **40%**

BONDS
- Corporate bonds
- Long-term government bonds
- Treasury bills
- Municipal bonds

15%   **30%**   **40%**

CASH
- CDs
- Money market funds

5%   **10%**   **20%**

*These hypothetical asset allocations illustrate varying levels of risk and are not intended as investment advice.

REBALANCING YOUR ASSETS

After you've decided on an allocation, you'll probably have to realign your portfolio from time to time to maintain it. If your stocks do particularly well in one year, for example, your allocation model will be more heavily weighed toward equities than it was originally, as the chart to the right illustrates. That means your portfolio will be potentially more volatile.

To rebalance, you can sell some stock and reinvest the money in bonds or cash, or you can add new investment money to those asset classes rather than to equities. Many mutual funds and variable annuity programs offer automatic rebalancing to make the task easier.

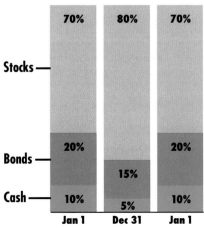

	Jan 1	Dec 31	Jan 1
Stocks	70%	80%	70%
Bonds	20%	15%	20%
Cash	10%	5%	10%

Stocks

Stocks are the key to growing an investment portfolio.

When you buy stock in a company, you become a **shareholder**, or stockholder. In effect, you own a piece of the company, even if it's a tiny sliver of the whole. The point of owning stock is that you share in the company's profits.

You can benefit two ways from owning stock. Many companies pay their shareholders **dividends**, or a percentage of their profits every year, usually in four installments. For example, if a company declares an annual dividend of $2 a share and you own 200 shares, you'll get $400 during the year.

More importantly, when the share price of stock increases, the value of your investment increases. For example, if you buy a stock when it costs $10 a share and the price increases to $20, your investment is worth twice what it was when you started. If you sell the stock at the higher price, you have a **capital gain**, on which you'll owe tax.

While you can never predict with certainty whether the price of any individual stock will go up or down, stocks in general have increased in value over time much faster than the rate of inflation. That's why stocks add growth potential to an investment portfolio, and are considered the most reliable method for substantially increasing the value of your assets over time.

A dollar invested in small company stocks on December 31, 1925, would have been worth $6,402.23 at the end of 2000, compared to $16.56, the value of a similar 75-year investment in U.S. Treasury bills.

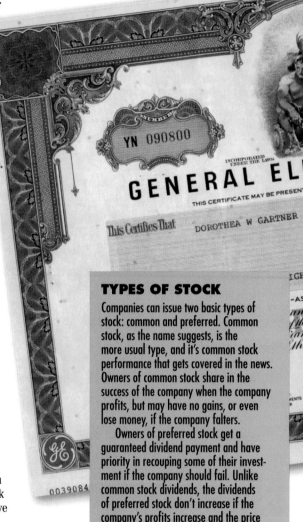

TYPES OF STOCK

Companies can issue two basic types of stock: common and preferred. Common stock, as the name suggests, is the more usual type, and it's common stock performance that gets covered in the news. Owners of common stock share in the success of the company when the company profits, but may have no gains, or even lose money, if the company falters.

Owners of preferred stock get a guaranteed dividend payment and have priority in recouping some of their investment if the company should fail. Unlike common stock dividends, the dividends of preferred stock don't increase if the company's profits increase and the price of preferred stock goes up more slowly.

THE VALUE OF STOCK

A stock's value is based on several things, including its price, its long-term growth potential, the dividends it pays, and the way it stacks up against other stocks.

Stocks don't have a fixed price. Rather, the price goes up or down based on what investors are willing to pay for it. The more people who want the stock, the higher the price is likely to go. Just the reverse occurs when lots of investors decide it's time to sell. That means the price will drop. Though sometimes prices change dramatically practically overnight, more typically there's a pattern of growth or decline over a period of days, weeks or months.

When you own something, it's also known as having **equity**.
That is why stocks are often known as equities.

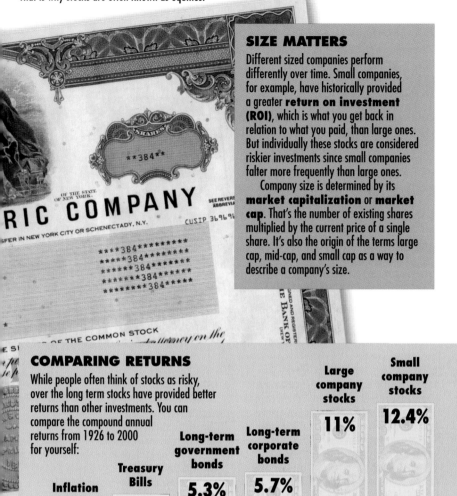

SIZE MATTERS

Different sized companies perform differently over time. Small companies, for example, have historically provided a greater **return on investment (ROI)**, which is what you get back in relation to what you paid, than large ones. But individually these stocks are considered riskier investments since small companies falter more frequently than large ones.

Company size is determined by its **market capitalization** or **market cap**. That's the number of existing shares multiplied by the current price of a single share. It's also the origin of the terms large cap, mid-cap, and small cap as a way to describe a company's size.

COMPARING RETURNS

While people often think of stocks as risky, over the long term stocks have provided better returns than other investments. You can compare the compound annual returns from 1926 to 2000 for yourself:

Inflation	Treasury Bills	Long-term government bonds	Long-term corporate bonds	Large company stocks	Small company stocks
3.1%	3.8%	5.3%	5.7%	11%	12.4%

Source: Ibbotson Associates, 2001. See page 153.

Ideally, you buy a stock when its price is poised to climb, so that you benefit from growth. Then you can sell it for the capital gain or hold it in your portfolio to increase your net worth.

CHOOSING STOCKS TO BUY

Different types of stocks serve different functions in your investment portfolio. The types you choose to buy depend on the role you expect the stocks to play. If you are interested in income from your equity investments, you might buy big brand names like General Electric or Walt Disney, because these companies have a history of paying consistent dividends. If you're interested in having your principal grow as much as possible, or what's known as maximizing **capital appreciation**, you might consider companies that reinvest most or all of their profits in order to expand and strengthen their business.

HOW YOU BUY

You can buy stock by calling your stockbroker or the brokerage house where you have an account, by using your online brokerage account, or in many cases directly from the company.

Buying directly, through what's known as a **dividend reinvestment plan**, or **DRIP**, you can use your earnings to buy additional shares and you can make additional lump-sum investments regularly, using a form the company sends when it announces dividend payments.

Most stock purchases are made in lots of 100 shares, known as **round lots**, but with a DRIP you can invest fixed amounts, say $100, and buy fractional shares.

Bonds

Assets you invest in bonds can provide income.

When you buy a **bond**, you're actually lending money to a corporation, government or other institution for a specific **term**, or period of time. In exchange for the use of your money, the borrower (also known as the bond issuer) typically promises to pay you regular interest payments at a **fixed rate**, known as the bond's **coupon rate**.

HOW BONDS WORK

When you buy a bond at the time it is issued, you pay its **face value**, or set price, which is also known as **par** or **par value**. That's frequently $1,000, though certain bonds cost more and some may cost less. If you keep the bond until **maturity**, or the end of its term, you get the face value back.

During the term, though, a bond's price fluctuates constantly, moving above and below par. If you sell before maturity, you may get more or less than you paid. Similarly, if you buy after the issue date, in what is known as the **secondary market**, you may pay more or less than the face value. Or you may buy above par, and sell at an even higher price. But if you own the bond when it matures you will get back its face value no matter what you paid.

A bond's price in the secondary market is affected by the interest rate it pays. If its rate is less than the rate on bonds that are being issued currently, its price will drop. That's because investors can earn more with the newer bonds, so demand for the older ones drops. If a bond's rate is higher than the current rate, its price will usually go up because investors are willing to pay more in order to earn more.

LENDER

IN FOR THE TERM

Bond terms can range from **short** (usually less than a year) through **intermediate** (two to ten years) to **long** (ten years or more). In general, the longer the term, the higher the coupon rate, because the issuer must make it worth your while to tie up your money for a longer period of time.

BOND APPEAL

Some investors buy high-rated bonds for the fixed income they provide, and often use the principal that's repaid at the end of the term to buy another bond. These investors simply ignore the bonds' price volatility, and think of them as a balance to equities in their portfolios.

TYPES OF BONDS

Bonds are issued by several different types of organizations, including:
- **Publicly held corporations**
- **Federal, state, and local governments**
- **Government agencies**
- **International corporations and governments**

Corporate bonds
These taxable bonds are the major source of corporate borrowing. You can buy **debentures**, backed by the general credit of the corporation, or **asset-backed bonds**, backed with corporate assets, such as property or equipment. Corporate bonds are priced at $1,000, though you may pay more or less than that amount for a specific bond after original issue.

Municipal bonds
These bonds are issued by state and local governments, often to fund work in a community, such as building roads and schools. Generally municipal bonds cost $5,000 and up, though they are sometimes available at $500. The big attraction of municipal bonds is that the interest is exempt from federal income taxes, and from state and local taxes in the state where they are issued.

BOND LIQUIDITY

A bond's liquidity, or the ease with which you can convert it to cash, depends on its term and type.

Short-term Treasury bills are generally the most liquid, and **zero-coupon bonds**, which are sold for less than par value, are the least liquid.

If liquidity is an issue, it's probably best to have a mix of maturity lengths in your bond portfolio, so that the principal on some of them will be available if you need cash.

When you buy a bond, you loan your money.

BORROWER

You receive regular interest payments until the term ends. Then the face value is returned.

Others take a less conservative approach, and buy and sell bonds to take advantage of the potential for capital gains. Both strategies work, but most investors concentrate on one approach or the other.

BOND RATINGS

To help you assess the credit risks involved in buying a bond, you can check the rating assigned by Standard & Poor's or Moody's Investors Service. To do the evaluation, these companies look at the type and amount of debt the issuer has and other factors, such as company revenues, its profits, and the general state of the economy. Then they assign a value from triple A to C. Any bond rated Baa or higher by Moody's and BBB or higher by Standard & Poor's is considered investment grade, or likely to pay as promised.

Low-rated bonds, sometimes known as junk bonds or high-yield bonds, are riskier but they also provide a higher rate of return. Some experts consider these bonds appropriate for a retirement-savings portfolio where any earnings can accumulate tax-deferred.

U.S. Treasury issues are not rated since they are backed by the "full faith and credit" of the federal government. The assumption is that they are solid investments, although their prices fluctuate the way other bond prices do.

U.S. Treasury notes

These bonds have intermediate (2 to 10 years) terms. They are issued by the government and considered to have the highest credit quality of any bond. These bonds are sold in units of $1,000 and can be purchased through a system known as Treasury Direct, run by the U.S. Treasury's Bureau of the Public Debt. The interest is exempt from state and local but not federal taxes.

U.S. Treasury bills

These are short-term instruments, with maturities of 4, 13, or 26 weeks. Your initial investment must be $1,000, and you can make additional investments in similar increments. Treasury bills offer maximum safety but usually lower return than longer-term bonds. You can also buy them through Treasury Direct, and the interest is exempt from state and local but not federal taxes.

Agency bonds

Federal, state and local agencies issue bonds, including those by mortgage associations. The most famous are Ginnie Mae, Freddie Mac, and Fannie Mae. The prices for agency bonds vary greatly, from $1,000 to $25,000. While the risk level is somewhat higher than for Treasury issues, the rates tend to be higher. The interest on mortgage bonds is fully taxable. Other agency bonds are exempt from state and local but not federal taxes.

Mutual Funds

Mutual funds can make investing more affordable and less intimidating.

When you buy a mutual fund, your investment is pooled with money from other investors and managed by a professional. Most funds own a large number of securities, providing a more diversified portfolio than most people can assemble on their own.

CHOOSING FUNDS

Mutual funds are tailor-made for building a portfolio because you can make regular investments with relatively small amounts of money—sometimes as little as $25 if you commit yourself to having the amount direct-deposited. To decide which types of funds and then which specific funds are right for your investment portfolio, you should examine a fund based on three characteristics:

Performance: How has the fund fared over time? What is its return over one year compared to over five years? Ten years?

Risk: How much volatility are you taking on with your fund? Remember: The longer your investment timeframe, the more risk your portfolio can tolerate.

Costs: Some funds are **no-load**, which means you pay no sales charge when you buy, reinvest or sell shares. With **load funds**, you pay a sales charge, or percentage of the price, to buy or sell, and sometimes to reinvest. A number of funds, described as **multiclass**, let you choose between paying when you buy or when you sell.

You pay **management** and **operating fees** to cover running the fund, and sometimes **distribution fees**, or 12b-1 fees, for marketing and advertising expenses. Each fund's fees are listed in its prospectus.

OPEN- AND CLOSED-END FUNDS

You may hear funds described as **closed-end** or **open-end**. Open-end funds, known as mutual funds, sell shares to new investors and will redeem shares at their **net asset value (NAV)**. Closed-end funds, also called **exchange-traded**

Mutual funds are collections of stocks, bonds or other securities owned by a group of investors and managed by a professional advisor.

Every mutual fund is created with a specific objective in mind, which typically fits into one of three models: growth, income, or a combination of growth and income. How a fund achieves these goals depends on the mix of securities within the fund. For example, a fund geared towards producing income would own mostly income instruments, such as bonds. A growth fund would own stocks. The securities the fund owns are known as its **underlying investments**.

funds, offer a fixed number of shares, and are traded like stocks on major stock exchanges. The share price rises and falls with investor demand and may be higher or lower than the NAV.

WHAT'S A FUND WORTH?

NAV is determined by adding up the value of all of the fund's holdings and dividing by the number of shares. When you buy a no-load fund, you pay the NAV for each share. The price of a load fund is usually quoted as its **MOP**, or **maximum offering price**. That's the NAV plus the sales charge.

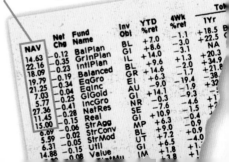

NAV	Net Chg	Fund Name	Inv Obj	YTD %ret	4WK %ret	1Yr %ret	
			BL	+7.0	-1.1	+18.5	B
14.63	-0.12	BalPlan	GI	+8.6	-3.0	+22.5	
22.16	-0.35	GrInPlan	IL	+14.0	-3.1	NA	
18.09	-0.23	IntlPlan	BL	+9.6	+1.3	+34.9	
19.79	-0.19	Balanced	GR	+14.6	-2.0	+21.8	
21.25	-0.34	EqGro	EI	+6.3	-1.7	-38.	
7.03	-0.04	EqInc	AU	-9.0	-19.4	+32	
5.77	-0.25	GlGold	GI	+14.1	-1.9	+	
27.36	-0.41	IncGro	NR	-0.3	-9.3	+1	
11.45	-0.28	NatRes	SE	-7.6	-4.6	+1	
15.00	-0.28	Real	GI	+10.9	-1.5	+2	
6.69	-0.06	StrAgg	MP	+6.3	-0.4	+	
5.59	-0.02	StrConv	BL	+9.0	-0.9	+0	
6.31	-0.05	StrMod	UT	+7.2	-4.0		
14.88	-0.15	Util	GI	+6.5	+1.		
	-0.08	Value	IM	+1.8	+1		

PICK AND CHOOSE

You can choose from among more than 8,000 mutual funds, which fit into a number of different categories.

INVESTORS

FUND MANAGER

INVESTMENTS

KNOWING WHAT YOU WANT

You can also buy mutual funds to serve particular investment purposes.

Index funds mirror a specific market average, like the S&P 500-stock index or the Lehman Brothers Treasury bond index. Index fund fees tend to be lower than those on other funds because there's little buying and selling.

Green funds attract investors interested in socially responsible investing. For example, green funds may avoid companies that manufacture or sell certain products, or seek out companies with strong environmental records.

Sector funds focus on a specific industry like technology or healthcare. The risk level is considered greater because the fund's performance depends on the activity of a single industry, which may enjoy a boom or get stuck in a downturn.

Aggressive growth funds seek long-term growth and invest in stocks that pay little or no current income, including new and less predictable companies and industries, or sometimes those that have fallen out of favor or hit hard times.

Growth funds seek above-average growth and pay little current income. They invest in companies with strong growth potential or a history of growing earnings. These types of funds invest in companies of all sizes, though some specialize in small- or medium-sized companies.

Growth and income funds, which include growth and income, equity-income, and balanced funds, seek a combination of current income with long-term growth. These funds invest in companies with strong growth potential, those that pay solid dividends, or in a combination of stocks and bonds.

Income funds seek a stream of current income by investing in income-producing securities, such as dividend-paying stocks, bonds or a combination of the two.

International stock and bond funds seek to profit from strong markets and industries abroad. **Global funds** invest in both international and U.S. securities. Depending on the makeup of the fund's portfolio, these funds have an added element of currency risk and the risk of economic problems in certain geographical areas.

Bond funds seek to provide current income by investing in corporate, government or municipal bonds. A fund's earnings are linked to the ratings and average maturities of the bonds it owns, since short-term, high-rated bonds typically pay less interest than long-term or low-rated ones.

High-yield funds can provide substantial income though they can also decline in value. These funds invest primarily in low-rated corporate bonds, also known as junk bonds. Tax-free high-yield funds seek similar goals by investing in low-rated municipal bonds.

Money market funds are the safest funds for preserving principal, and pay income based on current interest rates. These funds typically invest in short-term government and corporate debt, and tax-exempt funds invest in short-term municipal debt. Many of these funds offer check writing privileges.

Real Estate

Real estate is not just a roof over your head.

Investing in real estate can be another way to diversify your investment portfolio. Real estate investments come in all shapes and sizes. You invest in your home when you buy it, and you invest more when you fix it up. You can find partners and invest in rental apartments or commercial projects. You can invest in a **real estate investment trust (REIT)**, which resembles a closed-end mutual fund. Or you can buy raw, or undeveloped, land with the hope that you or someone else will build on it.

USING LEVERAGE

When you borrow money to pay for an investment, you are **leveraging** your investment. Leveraging means using a little of your own money to buy an asset that's worth a great deal more. For example, you might make a down payment of $20,000 on a $200,000 building, and sell it for $300,000.

You've taken less risk than if you paid the full price. And while you pay interest on the borrowed amount, what you get back for what you invested, called your **return on investment**, is much higher.

The danger of leveraging—whether you're buying real estate or anything else—is that if the property loses value, you can end up owing money on an investment that doesn't return a profit, and you can lose more than you borrowed.

The Upside

Many financial planners recommend adding some type of real estate to your portfolio as a diversifier.

- Real estate is a hedge against inflation, because it's an asset that generally increases in value when inflation rises

- The real estate market often zigs when the stock market zags. In other words, property values may increase as stock prices decline

- Some kinds of real estate provide tax advantages

- Property can increase dramatically in value and be sold at substantial profit

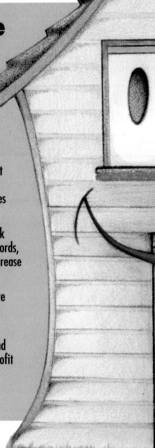

LIMITED PARTNERSHIPS

With a **real estate limited partnership**, or **RELP**, you invest in a company that buys and manages different kinds of properties, often of a particular type like shopping malls, warehouses or apartment buildings. Several limited partnerships can group together to buy larger properties, which in turn may mean greater profits for the investors. Private limited partnerships are generally restricted to high-asset investors and have a limited lifetime, generally 8 to 12 years. There are some real drawbacks. RELPs often impose large fees and are virtually impossible to get out of before the term expires. While they were once valued as tax shelters, that benefit has mostly disappeared.

BUYING TOGETHER
Real estate investment trusts, or **REITs**, are popular ways to invest in real estate without bearing the financial and physical burdens of owning property on your own. With a REIT, you invest in a group of properties or mortgages on properties owned and managed by an investment company.

A REIT, like a closed-end mutual fund, is established with a pool of money raised from a number of investors and invested by the company that manages the REIT. After it's set up, its shares are listed on an exchange and traded like stock. The price moves up and down in response to market conditions and changes in the real estate's value. The long-term profitability of the REIT depends on the underlying value of the property and quality of the management team.

While all REITs share basic characteristics, there are three different types: equity, mortgage, and hybrid. **Equity REITs** buy property that produces income or has growth potential. Some equity REITs focus on specific kinds of property, like industrial or office property. **Mortgage REITs** invest in real estate loans and start-up offerings. **Hybrid REITs** combine the equity and mortgage REIT approaches, owning and managing properties, as well as investing in real estate financing.

Most experts recommend choosing a well-established REIT with a track record you can examine, rather than one that's in the process of being established.

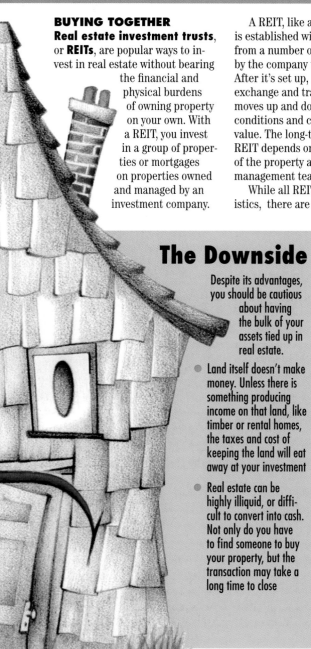

The Downside

Despite its advantages, you should be cautious about having the bulk of your assets tied up in real estate.

- Land itself doesn't make money. Unless there is something producing income on that land, like timber or rental homes, the taxes and cost of keeping the land will eat away at your investment

- Real estate can be highly illiquid, or difficult to convert into cash. Not only do you have to find someone to buy your property, but the transaction may take a long time to close

THE MORTGAGE ADVANTAGE
Using a mortgage to buy a home lets you build your investment in the property gradually at the same time that you're providing yourself and your family with a place to live. And since up to $500,000 of capital gains on the sale of your home are tax exempt if you're married, $250,000 if you're single, your investment can really pay off.

Experts caution that property values may not increase as dramatically in the future as they have in the past, however, leaving you short if you've counted on being able to afford retirement on income from selling your home. Another reason not to think of your home primarily as an investment is that the great majority of people—perhaps you included—prefer to stay where they are after they retire.

REVERSE MORTGAGES
If you own your home, you may be able to convert it to a source of retirement income by taking a loan known as a **reverse mortgage** from a bank or other lender. There are some drawbacks to these loans, however. They are often costly to arrange, the amount you receive may be quite small, the loan plus interest has to be repaid, and your equity in the property is gradually reduced.

Dollar Cost Averaging

You can spread out your investing and reduce its cost at the same time.

Some people spend lots of time trying to figure out the best time to invest, or trying to **time the market**. They believe they can identify when the market is low or a stock is selling at its cheapest price. They think they can pinpoint when the market is high so they can sell and make more money than the next person. While that sounds like a great idea, it's impossible to predict what the market is going to do.

A better strategy is to make investments on a regular basis, every month or every quarter. Since the price of securities fluctuates every day, buying at regular intervals means you will buy shares at a variety of prices, sometimes high, sometimes low. If you're investing $100 a month in a mutual fund, for example, you buy fewer shares of the fund when the price is high. When it is low, you buy more shares.

With this approach, called **dollar cost averaging**, you may not get the best or worst price of a fund, but over time you reduce the **unit cost**, or price per share, of your investment in that fund.

SETTING IT UP

With some investments you can have money moved from your checking or savings account to make a purchase each month.

Automatic investment plans are particularly good at helping you budget your money and allowing you to build a substantial portfolio over time rather than having to come up with larger sums at specific times—to meet an IRA contribution deadline, for example.

As an added bonus, you can usually choose to invest in smaller amounts than you could if you were writing a check—sometimes as little as $25 a time rather than the more typical $100.

You can use this tactic when you have a lump sum to invest in a variable annuity.

Averaging at work

When the price of a mutual fund share is low, your investment will buy more shares. When the share price is high, the same investment will buy fewer shares. And if you invest equal amounts, your average cost per share will be less than the average price per share. For example, if the average price of a share is $38 over five months, your average cost per share will be $37.86. If the prices are more volatile, the savings per share can increase. But over time, even small savings can contribute to building a larger portfolio.

Share price — 40 — 39 — 38 — 37 — 36 — 35

	JULY	AUGUST
Amount invested	$500	$500
Average share price per month	$41	$35
Number of shares purchased	12.20	14.29

THE AVERAGE SHARE PRICE

for example

$$\frac{\text{Average share price per month}}{\text{Number of months}} = \text{Average share price} \qquad \frac{(\$41+\$35+\$38+\$36+\$40)}{5} = \$38 \text{ Average share price}$$

With an annuity, you determine how your money is to be allocated among specific investment portfolios offered by the issuer. By having money moved from a money market account into these investment portfolios on a regular basis, such as monthly or quarterly, you can take advantage of dollar cost averaging in order to reduce the unit cost of shares in the investment portfolios, and avoid the potential risk of buying all your shares at the highest price.

THE IMPACT OF TIME

Dollar cost averaging can save you money in the short term. And like most investment strategies, the effect of regular investing multiplies over the long term.

For example, if you invest $166 a month for 30 years (or an annual total of $1,992, and $59,760 over the term), earn an 8% return, and reinvest your earnings, your investment account will be worth $244,692.

A WORD TO THE WISE

Dollar cost averaging is a smart way to invest, but that doesn't mean it's perfect. It doesn't assure a profit or protect against loss in a declining market. There's no guarantee that you couldn't make a large lump sum purchase at the lowest price so that your investment costs less than it would if you paid the average price over a period of time. And finally, you have to continue to invest even when prices drop if you're going to achieve your goal of reducing your average cost per share.

TRY IT WITH STOCKS

Dollar cost averaging is used most often with mutual funds and the investment portfolios in variable annuities, but the principle applies to stock investing as well, if you use a dividend reinvestment plan or a direct purchase plan to make regular additional investments. Though there may be a limit to the total amount you can invest at any one time, it's usually in the range of several thousand dollars.

In most cases there's only a minor fee for purchases you make directly—less than even the most modest brokerage sales charges. And with direct investment, as with dividend reinvestment, you can buy fractional shares, so all of your money is invested.

	SEPTEMBER	OCTOBER	NOVEMBER
	$500	$500	$500
	$38	$36	$40
	13.16	13.89	12.50

YOUR AVERAGE SHARE COST

for example

$$\frac{\text{Total amount invested}}{\text{Total shares purchased}} = \frac{\text{Average}}{\text{share cost}} \qquad \frac{\$2,500}{66.04} = \frac{\$37.86}{\text{Average share cost}}$$

Making the Most of Favors

Believe it or not, sometimes you get a break on your taxes.

Investing for retirement is different from any other type of investment for one big reason. There's a great **tax deferral** incentive built in. Tax-deferred investments allow you to postpone the taxes on earnings, and in some cases on the amount you're investing as well. Deferral not only delays the tax bite, but gives your money's growth a boost because compounding has a bigger base on which to work its magic and, in the best of circumstances, a long time frame.

HOW TAX DEFERRAL WORKS

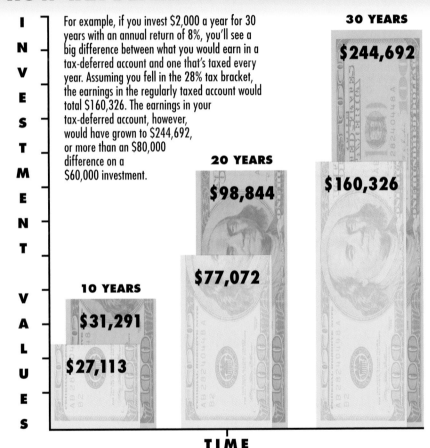

INVESTMENT VALUES

TIME

For example, if you invest $2,000 a year for 30 years with an annual return of 8%, you'll see a big difference between what you would earn in a tax-deferred account and one that's taxed every year. Assuming you fell in the 28% tax bracket, the earnings in the regularly taxed account would total $160,326. The earnings in your tax-deferred account, however, would have grown to $244,692, or more than an $80,000 difference on a $60,000 investment.

10 YEARS
$31,291
$27,113

20 YEARS
$98,844
$77,072

30 YEARS
$244,692
$160,326

CHOOSING INVESTMENTS

Are the investments you choose for a tax-deferred plan different from investments you'd pick for your other accounts? The answer is yes and no.

All long-term investment portfolios need to grow. That means focusing on equities, specifically stocks and the mutual funds and variable annuities that invest in stocks.

You need diversification in your tax-deferred plans as well. Since equity markets go through cycles, when some types of stocks turn in stronger performances in one phase and other stocks shine in another, being diversified helps even out the ups and downs.

The eventual tax you'll pay on your tax-deferred earnings—at the same rate you pay on other income, rather than at the lower capital gains rate—may influence the types of equities you stress, though. Some experts suggest choosing those that pay little current income but may provide strong growth in taxable accounts, while buying those that produce income as well as growth in your tax-deferred plans.

You might also consider high-yield bond funds, which can produce a lot of income. But it's smart to avoid municipal bonds in a tax-deferred plan since the interest they pay is tax exempt in a taxable portfolio but becomes taxable when you own the bonds in a tax-deferred plan.

MOVING THINGS AROUND

Another advantage of tax-deferred plans is that you can transfer assets among the investment accounts without owing tax on any gain in value. That's not the case with taxable investments.

For example, if you own shares in a mutual fund that has increased in value and you **liquidate**, or sell off your shares in the fund, you'll owe capital gains tax on your profit. But if you have shares in an equity investment portfolio in a variable annuity, you can move your investment out of that portfolio and into another one offered through the annuity without paying any tax on any increase in value until you withdraw.

You can do the same thing with investments in IRAs, 401(k)s, SEPs, and other tax-deferred plans.

ROLLING THEM OVER

You can move your tax-deferred investment plans from one trustee or provider to another and preserve their tax-deferred status. The process is called a **rollover** or transfer in some instances and a non-taxable **exchange** in others, depending on the plans in question.

For example, if you leave an employer where you had a 401(k) plan, you can roll over your investment into a 401(k) at your new employer or into an IRA, continuing to defer your tax burden until you start to make withdrawals. Similarly, you might want to invest your IRA in a variable annuity to take advantage of being able to arrange to have regular income distributed over your lifetime.

If you want to exchange a variable or fixed annuity contract provided by one issuer for a contract offered by another, you can do that too. The transaction, known as a 1035 exchange, is named for the section of the Internal Revenue Code that makes it nontaxable.

ROLLOVER
401(k) → IRA

ROLLOVER
IRA → IRA (Annuity)

1035 EXCHANGE
Annuity A → Annuity B

PAYING THE PIPER

When you do start to make withdrawals from your retirement accounts, you'll owe tax on the earnings as you withdraw them. If contributions were also tax-deferred, as they would be in a qualified plan, you'll owe tax on the total amount you withdraw.

In some cases, all of your earnings are paid before you begin to get your principal back. But with a nonqualified annuity, you can choose an income plan that returns some of your premium with each withdrawal, reducing the tax you owe.

TAX-EXEMPT INVESTING

If tax-deferred is good, tax-exempt can be better. Certain retirement vehicles allow you to accumulate earnings and never pay any tax on your withdrawals.

The classic tax-exempt investments are municipal bonds issued by state and local governments. The interest is exempt from federal tax and exempt from state and local tax if you live within the locality where they are issued. For example, a resident of Virginia pays no state tax on a bond issued there, though would owe state tax on a bond issued in Tennessee.

In 1997, Congress created a tax-exempt IRA, called a Roth IRA for Senator William Roth (R-DE), who pushed for its passage. With the Roth IRA, investors contribute after-tax dollars to the account. As long as the Roth IRA remains open for five years and you're older than age 59½ when you withdraw, the earnings are tax-free.

There are some limits with Roth IRAs. Your contribution is capped at the limit that applies for that year, though you can roll over your existing IRAs into a Roth. There are also income limits, so that you can't contribute to a Roth if you have an adjusted gross income of more than $110,000 if you're single or a combined income of more than $160,000 if you're married.

Creating an Income Stream

Investment income depends on the amount and the variety of your investments.

The amount of income your investments will provide after you retire depends on how much you've socked away over the years and the kind of return your investments pay.

LOOKING AT SPECIFICS

In this example, Bob and Mary have an income of $75,000 a year before they retire. Since experts estimate that they need 80% of their current income to maintain a similar standard of living, they'll need income of roughly $60,000 from various sources.

Assume they'll receive $15,000 a year from Social Security and another $15,000 in pension income. That means even in the first year of retirement, before inflation is a real factor, they'll have $30,000 less than they need.

Depending on the investments they've made, they'll either have access to enough income to meet their living expenses and have something left for pleasure, or they'll have to take other steps, including continuing to work, cutting back where they can, eating into principal or selling their house.

Assuming that they have accumulated assets worth $250,000, here's a look at the income it could produce if it were allocated in different ways. However, remember that these allocations are hypothetical illustrations and are not intended to predict the return on specific investments.

Bob and Mary have $250,000 in bank certificates of deposit (CDs) earning interest of 4% a year, or a total of $10,000. Since that amount does not meet their income needs, they'll have to use some of the principal if they have no other investments.

CDs	$250,000
Annual interest	x .04
Annual income	= $ 10,000

Advantages
Their investment is insured against loss of principal (if they have accounts in different banks, none of them exceeding $100,000).

Pitfalls
Each time they use principal they have less to reinvest. Then the earnings decline because there is less principal to earn interest on. And if they took the entire $20,000 shortfall each year, the account would be exhausted in 12½ years. Inflation is a concern as well. If inflation rises above 4%, as it has in the past, it would erode the value of their earnings more quickly than interest can make them grow.

Bob and Mary have $250,000 invested in stocks returning 11% annually on average during their retirement. If they use the $27,500 in dividends and increase in value their investment produces, they'll be close to meeting their income needs.

Stocks	$250,000
Annual return	x .11
Annual income	= $ 27,500

Advantages
Equities have historically grown in value and have been less vulnerable to the effects of inflation than other investments.

Pitfalls
The past is not a predictor of the future. While stocks have performed strongly over time, they do have off years. If the value of the stocks were to drop, either because of a market correction or a problem with the underlying business, their return would also drop. Bob and Mary might have to sell more stock than the value of their gain to make up the difference, risk taking a loss on the price, and end up with a smaller nest egg.

VARIETY IS BETTER

Most experts suggest that when you are planning for retirement income, it's smart to diversify your income sources, just as you did when you were accumulating assets. The traditional mix of professionally managed retirement accounts is 60% of their total assets in equities and 40% in fixed income accounts. Or you might choose to keep 10% in cash.

Bob and Mary might invest their nest egg in other ways, including fixed or variable annuities, mutual funds, and real estate, and arrange to turn that investment into a source of income.

If Bob and Mary invest their $250,000 in long-term U.S. Treasury bonds, which have an average 5.3% return, they'll receive an annual income of $13,250. That's less than half of what they need to fill in the difference between their Social Security and pension and their projected living expenses.

Bonds		**$250,000**
Annual interest	x	.053
Annual income	=	$ 13,250

Advantages

Their investment is safe because it's an obligation of the U.S. government and the payments will be made on schedule.

Pitfalls

Inflation again. Because Bob and Mary are locked into the interest rates the various bonds in their portfolio pay, their buying power will be eroded if inflation rises to a significantly higher level. In addition, the principal amount, when returned, would have reduced value, though they could reinvest it in another similarly priced bond.

ANNUITIES

They could annuitize the assets in a deferred annuity or buy an immediate annuity that would begin paying income right away. If they selected a fixed payout, they would know from the start how much they would receive for the period of time they chose, which could be as long as their joint lifetimes. If they chose a variable payout, the amount of income would not be guaranteed, because it would be based on the performance of their investment portfolios. But they would be assured of some income throughout the term they chose. The advantage of fixed income is its regularity, while the advantage of variable is that it has the potential to increase over time.

MUTUAL FUNDS

They might arrange with a mutual fund company to pay out their $250,000 investment in regular installments for the next 20 years. The amount, which the mutual fund company would determine based on the return on the fund, should provide a basic income each year, which could increase if the fund enjoyed strong returns or decrease if performance slowed. In addition to a shortfall, the problem is that one or both of them could live longer than 20 years, outliving their assets.

REAL ESTATE

It's difficult to predict return on a real estate investment because it depends on where the property is, whether it's producing income, and how much they pay annually to keep it up. Unless they're invested in REITs, which may pay a healthy dividend, or in income-producing property such as apartments or timberland, real estate can be difficult to convert to a stream of cash.

DOING MENTAL ACCOUNTING

Another decision they have to make is whether they want to preserve some of the assets to provide income for the surviving spouse, transfer wealth to their heirs, or make gifts to charities. If those things are important to them, they can plan to withdraw from accounts designed for retirement income, such as IRAs and annuities, while holding on to investments such as stocks that have no built-in mechanism for liquidating assets.

Investment Allocation Models

There's a better way to produce lifetime income.

If you allocate your investments among a number of different types of securities, you balance your risk and increase the stability of your return.

Adding an annuity, for example, may be the only way to lock in a lifetime income portion of your retirement portfolio, and building up your equity holdings can help ensure that your assets grow.

The allocation model that's right for you depends on three factors: your time horizon, your risk profile, and the amount of return you need. Take a look at the annual returns that could be produced by different allocations of an investment portfolio totaling $500,000.*

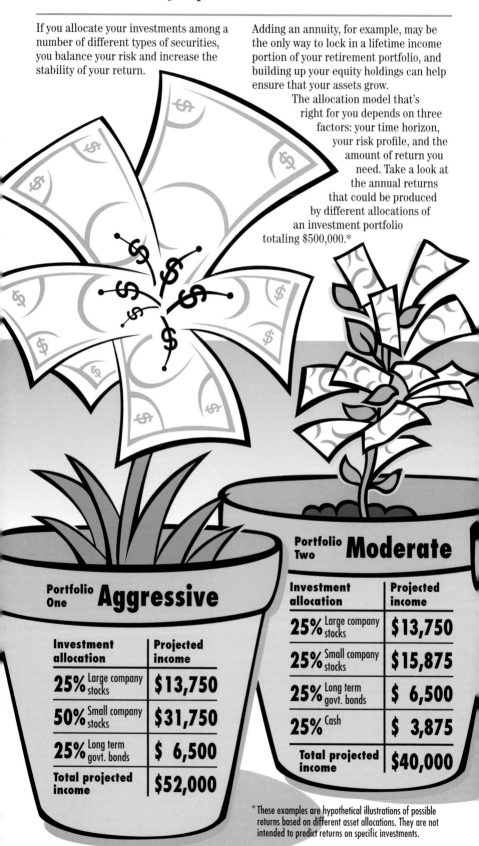

Portfolio One — Aggressive

Investment allocation		Projected income
25%	Large company stocks	$13,750
50%	Small company stocks	$31,750
25%	Long term govt. bonds	$ 6,500
Total projected income		**$52,000**

Portfolio Two — Moderate

Investment allocation		Projected income
25%	Large company stocks	$13,750
25%	Small company stocks	$15,875
25%	Long term govt. bonds	$ 6,500
25%	Cash	$ 3,875
Total projected income		**$40,000**

* These examples are hypothetical illustrations of possible returns based on different asset allocations. They are not intended to predict returns on specific investments.

COMPLICATING FACTORS

When you're ready to take income from your retirement portfolio, you must decide which investments to tap and which ones to leave alone. Your goals are to pay the least in taxes and protect more of your principal. This means weighing the benefits of the income from the asset versus the short- and long-term costs of using that money. Here are some of the things you may want to consider:

1. The taxes that will be due.

With taxable investments, earnings are taxed. If you postpone tax on your contribution to a qualified plan, tax will be due on the entire withdrawal amount. If you pay tax before purchase, only the earnings will be taxed. But with some withdrawal methods you'll receive all of your earnings first, before you begin to get the nontaxable portion back.

2. The accounts you're required to tap.

You must begin withdrawals from your traditional IRAs or qualified annuity plans when you reach age 70½, but not from annuity contracts purchased with after-tax dollars or Roth IRAs.

3. The growth potential of the investment.

You may choose not to withdraw from accounts that can continue to provide growth if they are left undisturbed.

INVESTMENT ALLOCATION MODELS

While the returns illustrated in these models may seem promising, keep in mind that the income is not guaranteed. In order to lock in income for your lifetime, you might consider buying a fixed annuity contract with part of your nest egg.

Portfolio Three **Conservative**

Investment allocation	Projected income
25% Large company stocks	$13,750
50% Long term govt. bonds	$13,000
25% Cash	$ 3,875
Total projected income	**$30,625**

MIXING IN ANNUITIES

Because they provide a number of pay-out options, including lifetime income, having annuities in your retirement portfolio can give you greater flexibility in managing your income.

For example, you could use a fixed income annuity to provide a stable monthly amount, which you could use to cover living expenses. Then income from other, less predictable sources, including stocks and variable annuities, could be used as emergency funds, to pay for extras, or to reinvest, allowing some of your assets to continue to grow.

You could use variable income annuities for their dual advantage of providing a hedge against inflation and paying a regular, although fluctuating, income. The amount changes, either on a monthly or annual basis, because it reflects the performance of the underlying investment portfolios. Over time, the general trend is for the amount to increase even if it declines in some periods.

The Possibilities of Annuities

You decide on the annuity features that put you on the right track.

Annuities are flexible, tax-deferred investment plans that you can use to help you achieve your long-term financial goals and provide a source of retirement income.

You can choose among different ways to buy an annuity, and you can set up a schedule for receiving income that suits your needs. With variable annuities, you can decide the level of investment risk you want to take, and select among a number of portfolios that match your income objectives.

When you've identified what you want an annuity to do for you, you can select a contract that's designed to do it.

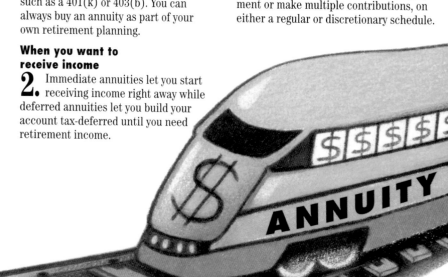

PUTTING IT TOGETHER

Buying the right annuity may seem intimidating because you have so many choices. But you can simplify the process by focusing on four decisions:

1. How the plan is offered

You may be able to choose an annuity as part of a qualified retirement plan such as a 401(k) or 403(b). You can always buy an annuity as part of your own retirement planning.

When you want to receive income

2. Immediate annuities let you start receiving income right away while deferred annuities let you build your account tax-deferred until you need retirement income.

3. The type of earnings you want

Some annuities provide you with income that never changes while others provide variable income payments based on the investment performance of the portfolios that you choose.

4. How you want to invest

You can buy an annuity with a single payment or make multiple contributions, on either a regular or discretionary schedule.

ANNUITIES

ONE LESS RESTRICTION
One appeal of nonqualified annuities, in addition to the choice of how you'll receive income, is that you can decide when you begin collecting it. You can start without tax penalty as early as 59½, as you can with IRAs. But unlike traditional IRAs, you can postpone past age 70½. The older you are when you begin, the larger your income will be. That means you can use it to cover a larger percentage of your expenses.

THE PLACE TO START
Here are some guidelines to help you begin to sort out what you want your annuity to do for you.

- Analyze whether money you may have in investments, CDs, or money market accounts could be working harder for your future
- Anticipate when you may want your retirement savings to begin providing income
- Decide how much you should be committing regularly to long-term retirement savings
- Compare the advantages of investments that have historically outpaced inflation with the security of a guaranteed rate of return

COMPARING ANNUITIES

Earnings in all types of annuities compound **tax-deferred** until you begin to take money out. That means you can build a larger retirement savings account than you would be able to if some of your earnings went to pay income tax every year.

When you're ready to draw on your retirement savings, all annuities offer you a number of options for receiving income. You can elect guaranteed lifetime income if you choose to **annuitize**, which means converting your retirement savings to a stream of regular payments.

Most variable annuities guarantee your principal if you die before you begin taking annuity payments. This is referred to as the **guaranteed death benefit**. Many contracts let you choose an **enhanced death benefit** that locks in your investment gains every few years or even every year.

A BRIEF CIRCULAR HISTORY
Annuity comes from the Latin word **annuus**, meaning yearly. Originally it referred only to a sum that was payable once a year. Today, the word annuity can mean both income paid on a regular schedule (an immediate annuity), and a type of retirement savings plan (a deferred annuity) that offers flexible purchase and withdrawal options, including—appropriately—one that pays income on a regular schedule.

Qualified Annuities

Annuities can be part of qualified retirement plans.

Money you contribute to an annuity program offered by your employer (as one of the investment options in a salary reduction retirement plan) reduces your current taxable salary in addition to accumulating tax-deferred earnings.

If you work for an educational, cultural or other nonprofit organization, you'll probably be able to choose either a fixed or variable annuity, or both, within your retirement plan. In addition, some companies have added annuities to their menu of retirement savings opportunities.

If you run your own small business, or work for yourself, you can invest in a qualified annuity by setting up a Simplified Employee Pension (SEP). A number of financial institutions, including banks and mutual fund companies, provide generic plans that you can adopt, or you can have a retirement specialist create a plan for you.

combination of those investments, generally allocating on a percentage basis. For example, in a **qualified variable annuity**, you might put 50% of your contribution into one equity investment portfolio, 25% into another equity portfolio, and 25% into a money market or fixed-income account.

In most plans you can move your money around among investments at least once a year. When you make a transfer, you don't owe income tax on your gains, but there may be fees for some switches. (After you retire, though, the switching restrictions may get tighter.)

EQUAL TREATMENT
If your employer offers a qualified plan, the eligibility rules have to be the same for every employee, from the boss on down—that's required by law. That includes the right to contribute the same percentage of your salary as other employees do and to have your contribution matched at the same rates, if your employer provides a matching plan.

Usually, you can join the plan once you've been on a job full time for a year, although some employers let you begin contributing right away. You should be alerted to your right to participate, but it often pays to ask as soon as you start working.

YOU MAKE THE CALL
Many qualified retirement plans are self-directed. That is, you choose where to put your money from the alternatives your employer offers. You can invest in any

WORKING A WORD HARD
Don't confuse **annuity**, the retirement savings plan, with **pension annuity**, the retirement income your employer pays. A pension annuity is usually a regular monthly check paid out of your employer's retirement fund. An annuity is a retirement plan that you can use both to accumulate savings and to provide a stream of income after you retire.

ANOTHER IRA

You can also open an IRA with an annuity provider and build an annuity-based plan. Then IRA stands for **individual retirement *annuity*** rather than individual retirement account. You're limited to the annual investment cap that applies to all IRAs except rollovers, and you're required to begin withdrawing when you reach 70½, but you can take advantage of the growth and payout options that annuities can provide.

The contribution cap is $3,000 for 2002 through 2004. It increases to $4,000 for 2005 through 2007, and reaches $5,000 in 2008. If you're 50 or older, you can also make annual catch-up contributions each year beginning in 2002.

You may be able to take a tax deduction for the contribution amount if you aren't eligible for an employer sponsored retirement plan or if your income is less than the current ceiling for deductibility.

However, to be sure you handle all the details correctly, you may want to consult your tax advisor or financial planner when you set up the plan.

MAKING COMPARISONS

Qualified	Nonqualified
Contribution limits	No contribution limits
Withdrawals must begin by age 70½ in most cases	No federal withdrawal rules but there may be state laws

A CLASSIC PLAN

Tax sheltered annuities, or TSAs, are classic salary reduction plans for teachers and healthcare workers. Qualified annuities, both fixed and variable, are among the most common investment choices in these plans. In many cases TSAs are used as supplements to defined benefit plans provided by employers, allowing the participants to build a substantial retirement fund. However, the employers don't necessarily make matching contributions.

While the tax-deferred attributes of an annuity provide no additional benefits by themselves, there can be a number of advantages to rolling over money in a qualified pension plan into a qualified variable annuity.

A QUALIFIED ADVANTAGE

Investment portfolios choice. Variable annuities typically offer a number of investment portfolios, so that you can choose those that are best suited to match your goals and your tolerance for risk.

Income opportunities. With an annuity, there's a well-developed system in place for providing a number of different income options after you retire, including those that provide lifetime income for you, or you and your spouse.

Insurance protection. The **death benefit** guarantees that if you die during the accumulation period, your beneficiaries will receive the greater of the amount of money that was invested or the contract's current value at the time of your death. Many variable annuities go even further and offer **stepped up benefits** that lock in investment gains every few years or even every year.

Nonqualified Annuities

You can buy a nonqualified annuity for your personal retirement portfolio.

If you are saving for retirement, a **nonqualified annuity** offers the benefit of tax-deferred earnings and the opportunity to receive a stream of income after you retire. What's more, these annuity contracts, sometimes called standalone annuities, have no contribution limits. That means you can add as much to your account as you choose in any year, either in incremental payments or a lump sum.

What's more, you can put income from any source into a nonqualified annuity, which means you can use gifts or an inheritance. And you're not required to begin taking income by age 70½, which can give you more control over your financial planning.

SOME THINGS DON'T CHANGE

Though there are some big differences between qualified and nonqualified variable annuities, they're alike in one key way—the investment portfolios they offer.

For example, if an annuity provider includes a dozen investment portfolios within a nonqualified annuity, those same accounts would usually be available to you in a qualified plan, or the other way around. That means that you have the opportunity to allocate your assets in similar ways.

THE USES THEY SERVE

You might purchase a nonqualified annuity to supplement the amount you're putting into an employer sponsored plan or, if you're self-employed, use a nonqualified annuity as a secondary source of retirement income.

Most financial advisors suggest that you invest the maximum allowed in your employer sponsored plan before contributing to a nonqualified annuity.

Because annuities may offer greater variety and flexibility than investments you can make in some employer plans, using them is a way to diversify your portfolio. For example, if you're part of an ESOP that puts your pension money into company stock, you might use a nonqualified annuity to put money into other types of

NONQUALIFIED VS.

AFTER-TAX $

After-tax dollars are what's left of your earnings after taxes are taken out. Contributions to nonqualified retirement plans are made with after-tax dollars. When you eventually take money out of nonqualified plans, you don't owe tax on the portion of the withdrawal that's considered return of principal. It has already been paid.

WAYS THEY'RE ALIKE

Tax-deferred earnings

Early withdrawal penalty

WAYS THEY'RE DIFFERENT

Invest after-tax dollars

No contribution limits

Income from any source

Flexible withdrawal rules

equity portfolios. Or if your defined benefit plan will pay you a fixed amount after you retire, you might put money into a variable nonqualified annuity that provides an opportunity for your annuity income to outpace inflation.

YOU'RE THE BOSS

The federal government doesn't require you to begin withdrawing from your nonqualified annuities when you turn 70½, as you must with a traditional IRA and many qualified retirement plans. Some states

QUALIFIED ANNUITIES

PRETAX $

Pretax dollars are what you earn before federal and state taxes are deducted. Contributions to qualified retirement plans are made with pretax dollars. That reduces the current income tax you owe, because your taxable income is reduced by the amount you invest. Eventually, though, you owe taxes both on the investment and the earnings when you take money out of the plan.

Tax-deferred earnings

Early withdrawal penalty

Invest pretax dollars

Contribution limits

Earned income only

Required withdrawal rules

have no age requirement either, while others impose mandatory withdrawals at some point, generally much later than 70½. And as these rules change, it's usually in your favor. For example, in 1998, New York pushed back its mandatory age for beginning withdrawals from 85 to 90.

ANNUITIES IN IRAS
You can usually buy annuities within your existing IRA. Many experts point out that the **death benefit** provision (which guarantees that if you die while still saving for retirement, your beneficiaries will receive at least the amount of your principal and often that amount plus locked-in investment gains), as well as the potentially strong performance of variable annuities, can make them a smart choice.

If you want to buy an annuity with your IRA contribution, you can select a contract that allows you to invest the amount annually that complies with IRS rules. When you're ready (but no later than age 70½), the annuity can be converted to an income stream which you can't outlive.

AN ANNUITY DEBATE
Some people question buying variable annuities in an IRA, since an annuity in an IRA or qualified plan does not provide any additional tax-deferred advantage beyond that provided by the IRA itself. These people maintain that you are adding a layer of additional fees to your IRA, which could make it harder to achieve the same return as you might otherwise earn, assuming you allocated your money in similar ways.

On the other hand, those fees go to pay for the insurance features of the contract, which many people think are valuable. You should weigh these insurance features, and whether or not the annuity gives you a broader range of investment choices, when you consider whether to fund a IRA or qualified plan with a variable annuity.

ROTH IRAS
Roth IRAs can provide tax-free retirement income if your account has been open at least five years and you're at least 59½ when you withdraw. But many experts agree they're not a substitute for variable annuities. Your contribution is limited to the annual IRA cap and you must have an adjusted gross income of less than $110,000 if you're single or $160,000 if you're married and file a joint return to be eligible to contribute.

Being able to save as much money as you can, and allow it to grow tax-deferred, may be a reason for the strong sales of nonqualified annuities. At the end of 2000, there was almost $1 trillion in assets tucked away in annuities. And with baby boomers marching toward retirement—by 2020, about 16.5% of the population will be over age 65—that amount is expected to grow.

Immediate vs. Deferred Annuities

The difference is all in the timing: income now
or income later.

If you buy an annuity, you can convert your
assets to income and receive that income
in regular payments. This feature distinguishes annuities from other individual
retirement plans, such as IRAs, which
require you to make withdrawals but don't
provide a guaranteed lifetime income
unless you have put the IRA assets into
an annuity.

Annuities also differ from other retirement plans because you can choose
between an **immediate annuity** if

WHAT YOU GET

The size of the monthly payment you'll
receive, on the other hand, is set by the
annuity provider based on

- The amount you use to buy the annuity,
  or **annuity principal**
- The payout option you choose
- Whether the annuity is fixed or variable
- Personal factors, including your age
  and, if it's a joint and survivor annuity,
  the age of the other person

IMMEDIATE ANNUITIES

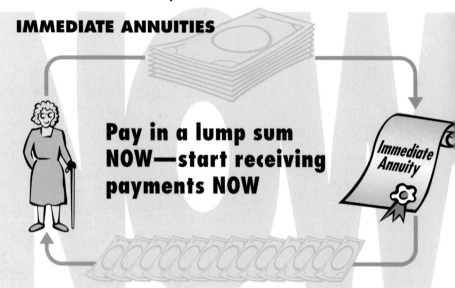

**Pay in a lump sum
NOW—start receiving
payments NOW**

Immediate
Annuity

you want the income right away and a
deferred annuity if you want to build
your account value over time and convert
it to income in the future.

THE IMMEDIATE APPEAL

Immediate annuities offer some advantages that can make them attractive
choices for retirement income.
Specifically, they can help ease the fears
people may have about managing a diversified investment portfolio or, even more
scary, of outliving their resources.

For example, someone who has just
received a large sum of money—an inheritance, a bonus, or profits from selling a
business—but really needs a steady
source of income can choose an immediate
annuity. In addition, many experts suggest
that anyone who expects a lump sum pension or 401(k) distribution should consider
an annuity as a way to convert their money
into a stream of income they can't outlive.

IMMEDIATE ANNUITIES

When you buy an immediate annuity, you
make a single lump-sum payment and set
the starting date for the payout to begin
sometime within the next 13 months—
generally sooner rather than later. The
term, or period of time that will be
covered, and the amount you'll receive
are laid out in the annuity contract.

With an immediate annuity, you
control the term: You can choose
income for your lifetime (known as a
life annuity), or for your lifetime and
that of another person (known as a **joint
and survivor annuity**) You can also add
a guarantee period to a lifetime income
payment option so that your beneficiaries
will receive the payments remaining in
the guarantee period if you die before the
end of the period. You can also choose
time-specific or amount-specific payout
possibilities.

CHOOSING A CONTRACT

In the past, many people chose a fixed immediate annuity for the predictable payments it promised. More recently, there's been increased interest in **variable immediate annuities**.

In choosing a fixed immediate annuity, the decision usually comes down to which highly rated provider will guarantee the largest regular income for the term you select. Income amounts vary because companies use different annuity purchase rates for determining their payments.

For example, a 55-year-old widow who buys a $100,000 immediate annuity, and elects to receive monthly payments for the rest of her life, might receive anywhere from $611 to $766 each month depending on the provider. If she lived for 35 years—

you must purchase with a lump sum, you can build your deferred account with a lump sum, a series of payments over time, or both. The ability to combine one-time and periodic contributions gives you added flexibility in building a larger retirement resource.

You continue to have access to your money in a deferred annuity until you convert your accumulated assets to a revenue stream. This means you can make some annual withdrawals, or surrender the contract entirely, getting back its current value minus any surrender fees. But if you do withdraw, the money will be gone, and your retirement account will be reduced. You may also have to pay a tax penalty if you're younger than 59½.

DEFERRED ANNUITIES

Save OVER TIME— start receiving payments LATER

Deferred Annuity

to age 90—the difference could amount to more than $65,000.

In choosing a variable immediate annuity, which guarantees income for life in amounts that will vary to reflect the performance of the investment portfolios you select, you look at a number of factors, including the performance of the investment portfolios in the contracts you're considering, the options offered, and the annual expenses of the contracts.

DEFERRED ANNUITIES

A deferred annuity gives you the opportunity to build your retirement savings over a period of years. What you're deferring is the moment you begin to receive income. But in the period between signing the contract and converting your accumulated assets to a revenue stream, your investment grows in either a fixed account, variable investment portfolios, or both.

Unlike an immediate annuity, which

IT CAN PAY TO WAIT

Deferred annuities are especially appealing if you've put as much into your employer's salary reduction plan as you can but want to put away more for your retirement. And if you aren't earning income, a deferred annuity is one way for earnings on your investment to grow tax-deferred.

There are no annual limits to the amount you can contribute to a nonqualified deferred annuity—as there are with employer sponsored plans and IRAs—so you can contribute more when you have more on hand, for example as the result of a big bonus, a short-term, high-paying job or other windfall.

THE TIME TO BUY

While you can buy a deferred annuity at almost any time, including after you retire, many experts advise that deferred variable annuities need to grow for a period of time before they really begin to pay off.

Fixed Annuities

Traditional annuities earn a fixed rate of interest
and pay a fixed income.

When you buy a **fixed deferred annuity**
contract, you get two promises from the
issuer: a fixed rate of return during the
build-up period while your retirement
savings grow, and many ways to receive retirement income, including payments that
are guaranteed to continue for as long as
you live.

The two promises are related. Your
money in the annuity grows tax-deferred
until you're ready to withdraw. The earn-

ings rate paid on your savings, the
amount you save, and the length of time
your annuity grows all determine the
income you'll receive. For many people,
the certainty of a fixed rate of return is a
chief attraction of fixed annuities.

Equally important, the rate you're paid
is guaranteed, regardless of whether
interest rates move up or down.

BUILD UP

SETTING THE RATE
The company that issues the annuity sets the
current rate of interest it will pay on its
contract with you and revises it periodically.
Rates may be adjusted monthly, annually, or
less frequently. When the rate changes,
it sometimes increases and sometimes
decreases, reflecting what's happening in the
economy at large. But it can never go below

the **guaranteed rate**—typically 3% to
4%—that's set when you buy the annuity.
In general, the new rate is based on the
return the company is earning on its own investment portfolio, typically government and
corporate bonds and residential mortgages.
The **spread**, or difference between what the
issuing company expects to earn and what it
commits itself to pay out, can help offset some
of its expenses and provide some of its profits.

You can comparison shop for earning
potential as well as for high ratings and
financial strength of the insurance company
providing the annuity. The fact that renewal
interest rates tend to be lower than introduc-
tory, or first year rates, can complicate your
comparison of earning potential. One solution
is to compare older polices as well as the new
ones offered by the same
insurance companies.

Current Rate

Guaranteed Rate

A SECOND CHANCE
Fixed annuities can have a **bailout
clause**, sometimes known as an escape
clause, that lets you surrender your policy
without penalty if the interest rate that's
being offered drops below a certain level,
often one percentage point less than the
previous rate, even if it's above the
guaranteed rate.

There are a couple of catches though:

Usually if an annuity's rate drops significantly, interest rates in general have
dropped. That means newly issued
annuities are likely to be paying at comparable levels to the one you're giving up.

And if you transfer your money to a
different type of investment or keep the
cash, and you're younger than 59½, you
may have to pay a 10% premature with-

HOW COMPANIES INVEST

The amount you invest to buy a fixed annuity contract goes into the provider's general account, along with premiums from other investors and other company revenues. Because the company has such large sums to invest, it can diversify its holdings and earn a better return on its investment for the same investment risk than you could investing on your own.

A potential downside to buying a fixed annuity may occur if the issuing company gets into financial difficulties, since its creditors have a right to assets in the general account. These situations are highly unlikely, however, since the insurance industry is heavily regulated and individual companies are rated regularly.

But be alert: Companies touting fixed annuity returns much higher than the rates offered by the competition may be

COMPARATIVE RATES

The more competitive the annuity market, the greater the likelihood that the interest rates on the plans you're considering will be attractive. Typically, the rates are on a par with what you'd earn on a long-term bond, and higher than what CDs and money market funds are paying.

too good to be true. Sometimes, promises of stellar returns are a red flag that annuity money is going into riskier investments, like junk bonds. Before buying, ask to see the rate that the issuing company has paid over the past ten years and be sure to check the company's ratings.

PAY OUT

SAFETY FIRST

Fixed annuities, sometimes called guaranteed annuities, are considered safe because you can count on receiving the specific return you're promised each year.

The guarantee is backed by the insurance company issuing the annuity, not the government.

But if you buy your contract from a highly rated company, its financial strength and reputation stand behind your contract.

Rating services such as Standard & Poor's, Moody's, A.M. Best, and Fitch rank annuity providers on their overall financial condition, which underlies their ability to meet their obligations. These reports are available in public libraries, on the Internet, from your financial advisor, and from the insurance company if you request it.

THE INFLATION ISSUE

The flip side of safety, or the guaranteed return, is that the amount you get does not increase with inflation the way that Social Security payments do. The major risk of any fixed income source is that your costs will increase over time, but the income you receive will not.

If inflation should increase rapidly, as it sometimes does, an income that was once

adequate may leave you short of cash. And the longer you live and continue to collect, the less far your income is likely to stretch even if inflation increases only modestly.

drawal penalty on your taxable earnings, plus whatever taxes are due. If you withdraw only part of the accumulated contract value, the federal government's rules say that you withdraw earnings first, not the principal. That means you could pay tax on the entire withdrawal amount.

EXTRA PROTECTION

All states have **state guaranty funds** to protect contract owners against the insolvency of an insurance company issuing insurance contracts, including annuity contracts. But there are limits on benefits and coverage set by state law.

More about Fixed Annuities

New annuity products and provisions are introduced regularly.

Over the years, insurance companies have increased the number and variety of annuities they offer. They have also added new provisions to their contracts to make them more flexible. So as people find themselves having to take more responsibility for providing the income they'll need after they retire, they can choose among a number of different products designed to provide that income. They also have increasing opportunity to change their minds as their circumstances change, though that privilege may involve some additional cost.

INDEXED ANNUITIES

An **equity-indexed annuity** makes it possible for retirement savers to benefit from potential gains in the stock market while still receiving the guaranteed minimum return promised by a fixed annuity. The basic principle is that if an index such as the S&P 500-stock index that tracks the performance of a certain group of stocks goes up, your account is credited with a return based on the percentage of the gain in that index. That happens at predetermined times during the annuity's life.

But if the market should experience a sustained fall in value, the advantage of an equity-indexed annuity is that you're still guaranteed an interest rate **floor**, or minimum earnings rate on your investment.

HOW EQUITY INDEXING WORKS

You can get a sense of how your investment can grow with an equity-indexed annuity in the

S&P 500 Index

High
Close
Low

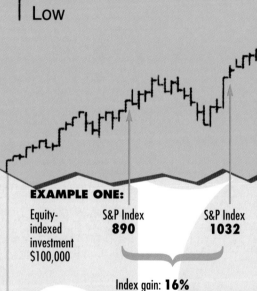

EXAMPLE ONE:

Equity-indexed investment $100,000	S&P Index **890**	S&P Index **1032**

Index gain: **16%**

Participation rate:	x **80%**
Equity index gain:	= 12.8%
	(80% of 16%)
Interest credited:	**$12,800**
	(12.8% of $100,000)

WHAT TO LOOK FOR

Since it can be difficult to compare equity-indexed annuities offered by various annuity companies, you can ask these questions to help you choose:

What do I earn in the annuity when the market goes up? What's known as the **participation rate** typically ranges from 50% to 100% of the index price gain (excluding dividends) and can be different for different contracts.

Is there a cap, or maximum amount of interest, that will be credited annually? Some companies limit the amount of index gain that will be added to your account. The caps may vary from company to company and vary from year to year.

What rate do I earn if the market drops? Check to see if the guaranteed rate is for the annuity's guarantee period or is adjusted annually.

What do I lose if I surrender my annuity early? Compare the surrender fees of the different products and how long they are in effect. Most are a percent-

following examples. Remember that in years when the index loses value, your account is credited with the minimum rate your contract provides.

The participation rate is one of the factors that helps determine your return on an equity-indexed annuity. Different contracts offer different rates.

EXAMPLE TWO:

Equity-indexed investment $100,000	S&P Index **890**	S&P Index **1032**
	Index gain: **16%**	
Participation rate:	x **60%**	
Equity index gain:	= 9.6%	
	(60% of 16%)	
Interest credited:	**$9,600**	
	(9.6% of $100,000)	

age of the assets, which decline over the first seven years and then disappear.

A TRADE-OFF
While the return on an equity-indexed annuity is based on the performance of a stock market index, you don't get the full boost of a rising market (or risk the full impact of a falling one). Instead, you get a percentage of the amount the index gains over a period of time, but not dividends, or net profits a company distributes to stockholders.

MARKET VALUE ADJUSTMENTS
Some fixed annuities, called **Modified Guarantee Annuities**, include a **market value adjustment (MVA)** feature. The adjustment is made if you want to surrender your annuity and possibly in situations where you access your money. You might make that choice if interest rates in general have increased and you want to purchase another annuity paying a higher rate—or if you need the money for any purpose. What the MVA does, in effect, is shift some of the investment risk from the company to you.

Because the annuity company has invested your premium to be able to pay you the rate guaranteed in your contract, it could lose money if it had to sell those investments at a discount to refund your premium plus your earnings. So it uses a fixed formula to figure the **adjustment**, or charge you must pay from your earnings, for taking money under these circumstances.

If you withdraw your premium when interest rates have dropped, you may receive the benefit of positive market action. Or, the annuity company could realize a gain when it sells the investments. Then the MVA formula may result in a positive adjustment to your withdrawal.

CONTRACTUAL ISSUES
Each contract may have different provisions, including whether it has the right to take some of your principal to make the adjustment or whether you are assured the right to keep at least a minimal percentage of earnings. It's something to factor into your purchase decision.

At the same time, you may find that the earnings rate offered by annuities with an MVA feature is higher than that offered by other annuities to compensate you for the potential risk you take.

Annuities with MVA factors also generally offer longer interest rate guarantee periods than other annuities.

Variable Annuities

Variable annuities offer investors more choices.

Variable annuities provide many of the benefits of fixed annuities—including tax-deferred earnings and a choice of payouts, plus the opportunity to make unlimited contributions if the annuity is nonqualified. In addition, they offer the potential for greater returns and the opportunity to make your own decisions about how to allocate your assets among investment categories.

With variable annuities, lots of things can vary, or change: the rate of return which you earn, the amount of income you receive if you annuitize, and how your money is invested. What remains constant with all annuities, fixed or variable, is the opportunity to select guaranteed lifetime income.

CREATING A PORTFOLIO

When you buy a variable annuity, you allocate your money among a number of **investment portfolios**, also called **subaccounts** or **variable accounts**. The accounts are just like mutual funds, either designed specifically for the annuity company or versions of existing funds designated for exclusive annuity use. Although the names of the investment portfolios may be the same or similar to those of retail mutual funds, they are not the same funds.

Your job is to choose among the ones that the issuing company offers, much as you would with a 401(k) or 403(b) retirement plan. Typically, there will be a dozen or more, including stock portfolios, a money market account, a government bond portfolio, a corporate bond portfolio, and a guaranteed account, which is similar to a fixed annuity investment. Sometimes, you have an even wider choice drawn from a number of different investment management companies.

MAKING THE INVESTMENT

You can allocate your money however you like, usually on a percentage basis: 50% in a growth stock portfolio, for example, 25% in a balanced portfolio, and 25% in a guaranteed or money market account.

Each time you add money, you buy a specific number of **accumulation units**, or shares, based on the **net asset value (NAV)** of the investment portfolio you're putting money into, adjusted for the annuity mortality and expense risk fee, or m&e (see page 134). The **accumulation**

How They Work

1. Choose a variable annuity

INVESTMENT $

unit value is the total value of the investment portfolio divided by the number of existing accumulation units.

GUARANTEED DEATH BENEFIT

Many investors are attracted by the death benefit variable annuities provide, which is based on the claims-paying ability of the insurance company that issues the contract. It means that if you die before you begin to receive income, your beneficiaries will receive, at the minimum, the amount you put into the annuity. With most contracts, in fact, investment gains are locked in regularly so that your beneficiaries receive more than your principal, even if the value has dropped back down at the time of your death. In contrast, a mutual fund pays your beneficiaries whatever your account is worth at the time of your death, even if it's less than the amount you invested.

IN THE BALANCE
You can weigh the advantages of fixed and variable annuities.

Variable	Fixed
Various levels of risk	Guaranteed returns
Greater potential rewards	No inflation protection
Choice of investment portfolios	Insurance company manager chooses investments
Assets in separate accounts	Assets in general accounts

THEY'RE YOURS

Variable annuities differ from fixed annuities in another important way. Your retirement savings go into individual accounts held in an issuer's **separate account**, rather than into its general account. (The exception is any money you put in a fixed account.) As a result, your retirement savings are shielded from the issuing company's creditors, As an extra bonus, some states protect your savings from your creditors as well.

2. Allocate money to investment portfolios

3. Adjust your allocation

4. Receive your payout

Stock

Money market

Government bond

Corporate bond

Guaranteed account

UNDERLYING INVESTMENTS

The portfolios you choose in your variable annuity are called your **underlying investments** because the performance of your annuity as a whole is based on how these investment portfolios perform. And the portfolios have underlying investments as well: the stocks or bonds they own. It is the collective performance of those stocks or bonds that determines the performance of the portfolio.

The assurance the death benefit provides can help stem your fear of losing money and encourage you to make more aggressive portfolio choices, thus increasing your chances of building a larger annuity value. In the same vein, the death benefit may also reassure people otherwise reluctant to invest in equities at all that they can afford to do so.

A BRIEF HISTORY

Variable annuities were introduced in 1952. Their history, like that of mutual funds and self-directed pension plans, is directly related to the increasing responsibility individuals have for making their retirement financially secure.

PUTTING MONEY TO WORK

When you add money to your variable annuity either in a lump sum or as **incremental purchases** during an accumulation period, you must decide how your assets are going to be allocated to the investment portfolios you have chosen.

With many variable annuities, you can allocate a specific percentage of your purchase to each of your portfolios at the time you buy. For example, if you invest $40,000 and have selected four investment portfolios, you might buy $10,000 worth of accumulation units in each of the portfolios. Or, if you invest $400 a month, $100 would go to each of the portfolios.

Another approach is to put the investment amount in a fixed or money market account within the variable annuity and arrange to have the assets moved gradually into one or more of your investment portfolios. That helps you avoid making a large purchase at what might turn out to be the highest price.

MAKING ADJUSTMENTS

Variable annuities let you create asset mixes that you're comfortable with, either at different stages in your life or in different economic climates. This flexibility lets you share in the benefits of a strong stock market, for example, or move money into more stable accounts if you're concerned about preserving your gains as you get closer to retirement.

No one mix suits every investor, though many investors emphasize stock portfolios, since they have provided the strongest returns over the long term, and thus the greatest opportunity for growth.

More about Variable Annuities

You call the shots on allocating your assets with a variable annuity.

Because they provide individual control over retirement savings, variable annuity contracts are more flexible and as a result more complex than fixed contracts. In exchange for giving you more options and choices, they require you to make more decisions.

MANAGING RISK AND RETURN

As with any equity investment, you risk loss of principal with a

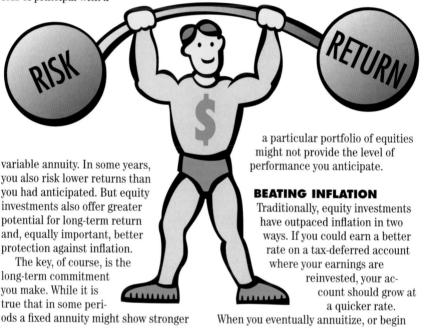

variable annuity. In some years, you also risk lower returns than you had anticipated. But equity investments also offer greater potential for long-term return and, equally important, better protection against inflation.

The key, of course, is the long-term commitment you make. While it is true that in some periods a fixed annuity might show stronger

gains than a stock portfolio, historically the longer that money is in equities, the greater the potential for growth.

Using the principle of **diversification**, which means that your investment portfolios are invested in many different companies and industries, helps protect you against sustained losses in a single stock or sector of the market. What it can't protect you against, however, is that

a particular portfolio of equities might not provide the level of performance you anticipate.

BEATING INFLATION

Traditionally, equity investments have outpaced inflation in two ways. If you could earn a better rate on a tax-deferred account where your earnings are reinvested, your account should grow at a quicker rate. When you eventually annuitize, or begin

UNDERSTANDING BENCHMARK RATE

If you choose a variable income option when you annuitize, the amount you'll receive is based on an **AIR**, or **assumed interest rate**. It's also referred to as a **hurdle rate** or a **benchmark rate**.

You may have the option of picking one of two interest rates—frequently 3% or 6%. That rate is used to determine the amount of the first income check you receive and is the standard, or benchmark, that's used to determine whether the checks that follow are more or less than the initial one. At 3%, the initial amount is lower, but there's the potential for a more rapid increase in what you receive and larger payments over time. At 6%, the initial amount is larger and you can expect increases to be more gradual.

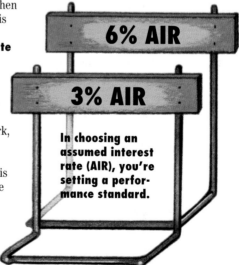

6% AIR

3% AIR

In choosing an assumed interest rate (AIR), you're setting a performance standard.

taking income, you'll probably have more money than you would have amassed with a more conservative choice.

Second, with variable annuities you can leave some or all of your retirement savings in growth accounts even after you begin to take income. That means the payments you receive can increase over time—though of course they can also decrease if investment performance slows.

USING BENCHMARKS

If you choose a higher **benchmark rate**, the amount of your first check will be larger than if you choose a lower rate. If your investment continues to produce a straight 6% return after the annuity and investment expenses (admittedly an unlikely prospect) your annuity income will stay the same. But any change, up or down, in the performance of your selected investment portfolios means you'll receive different amounts of monthly income over the time you collect. In some variable annuitization plans, the amount is adjusted annually and monthly payments throughout the year remain at the same dollar amount.

Your other choice—the lower benchmark—would produce a smaller initial payment. But you can anticipate larger increases in your monthly income when the performance of your chosen investment portfolios is strong, and you have more protection against a drop in income, since the market return is less likely to drop below the lower rate.

While committing yourself to a choice such as this may seem difficult, you can ask your investment advisor to track what's happened to variable incomes over the past ten years, and what a sustained drop in the underlying investments would mean to your income.

And you can turn to page 104 for a more detailed explanation of how your payout is figured, based on the number of **annuity units** in your account.

AN ADDED PLUS

Another major appeal of variable annuities is that you can make tax-free transfers among the portfolios your

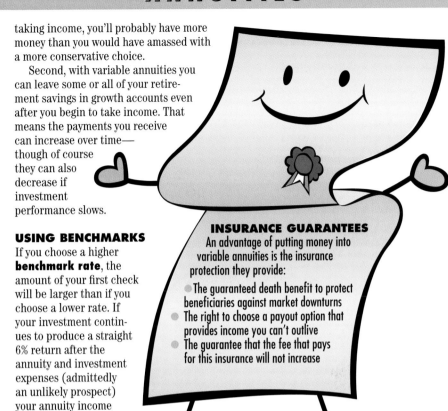

INSURANCE GUARANTEES
An advantage of putting money into variable annuities is the insurance protection they provide:

● The guaranteed death benefit to protect beneficiaries against market downturns
● The right to choose a payout option that provides income you can't outlive
● The guarantee that the fee that pays for this insurance will not increase

annuity offers. For example, if you're convinced it's time to increase the percentage of your retirement savings in more aggressive growth stocks, you can shift money from a balanced or money market portfolio. Or you might want to readjust your asset allocation from time to time. This flexibility lets you have continuing control over your retirement savings.

The earnings in the account you're taking money out of, which have grown tax-deferred, can be transferred without tax into the stock account.

MVAs IN VARIABLE ANNUITIES

Sometimes there may be a **market value adjustment (MVA)** on transfers from the fixed-income account of a variable annuity, to adjust for increases and decreases in interest rates. For example, if you wanted to transfer $10,000 from a fixed account to an equity portfolio prior to the maturity date, and after interest rates had gone up, you could move a portion of that amount, and the balance would go to the annuity provider. The terms of each contract can be different, so make sure you check them as part of your buying decision.

Purchase Plans

You can buy an annuity all at once, or little by little.

Having lots of choices can make investing intimidating. But variety can work in your favor, too, especially if it gives you flexibility in how you buy. That's because finding the money to invest or deciding how to invest it are big issues for most people.

For example, you might be able to commit a small amount each month to build your personal retirement savings, but not several thousand dollars at a time. Or you might get a $5,000 bonus and want to put it to work right away.

That's one of the reasons annuities can be appealing: You can choose a **flexible premium annuity** that lets you invest on a schedule that works for you, or you can buy a **single premium annuity** with a lump sum purchase.

SINGLE PREMIUM ANNUITIES

Most single premium annuities require a minimum investment, often $5,000, but impose no **ceiling**, or upper limit, on the amount of the purchase. That's one reason people who inherit a sum of money or receive a lump sum payment see these annuities as a logical choice.

Single premiums can be used to buy either immediate or deferred annuities, based on whether you want to begin to take the income quickly or at some point in the future. You can also choose between a variable annuity to take advantage of the opportunity to outpace inflation or a fixed annuity for its predictable rate of return and income stream.

COMBINATION PLANS

After you make your initial lump sum payment, some contracts, called modified single premium annuities, allow you to put additional money into the existing annuity. You may have the choice of building the account with other lump sum amounts or with periodic deposits as you would with a flexible-payment annuity. Other companies will require you to purchase a new contract to add more money.

Unless you're buying a contract you intend to annuitize right away, you should probably ask about add-on provisions before you commit yourself to a contract. That eliminates surprises if your plans or your circumstances change.

ONE CHECK AT A TIME

The other way to buy an annuity is by making contributions either on a regular schedule or one that suits your changing financial situation. After an initial investment, typically of $500 to $1,000, you might invest $100 a month, year in and year out. Or you might add whatever money you earn from an occasional part-time job.

Most contracts are flexible, so you can skip a month or vary the amount you contribute each year. The danger you face with sporadic contributions, however, is not committing enough to your long-term needs, and therefore potentially facing a shortfall after you retire.

To avoid this situation, you may want a fixed amount transferred automatically from your checking or money market account each month—sometimes in sums as modest as $25 a month. This approach usually commits you to regular contributions—but in most cases consistency is the most reliable approach to retirement savings.

AUTOMATIC TRANSFERS

INVESTING EARLY AND OFTEN

Making regular additions to your annuity can help to energize your retirement planning. The earlier you start, generally speaking, the easier it is to build the resources you need to supplement your income. And you can work with your financial advisor to figure out how much you need to save and what you should be earning on those savings to generate the level of income you'd like to be able to count on.

You can work with your financial advisor to figure out the amount you'll need to produce a specific monthly income.

In the following example, you can get a sense of what you would have to invest to receive $500 a month from a fixed annuity earning 6% annually, assuming you chose lifetime payments beginning at age 65.

LUMP SUM PLUS MONTHLY PAYMENTS

Invest between ages	Amount you need to invest
40 – 65	$123 each month
50 – 65	$293 each month
60 – 65	$1,223 each month

THE VARIABLE DIFFERENCE

With a variable annuity, you can't predict the contract value you will accumulate or the amount of income your savings will generate in the future. But most experts agree that if you were to put money into your investment portfolios at the levels of the fixed annuity example shown to the right, if most of those portfolios were invested in equities, and if you chose a variable payout, your initial income should be larger and should increase over time.

STOP

GO

STOP & GO

Rolling It Over

The point of a rollover is preserving an investment's tax-deferred status.

Once you've made the commitment to invest for retirement, it's important to keep the momentum going. Sometimes that means simply continuing to contribute. But there are times when you have to take certain steps to preserve your retirement fund. For example, you might get a distribution from a qualified retirement plan when you change jobs. Or your employer might end the plan.

Experts agree that you should move the money intact to another qualified plan to protect its tax-deferred status, ensure its continued growth and avoid the 10% early withdrawal penalty you might face if you're younger than 59½.

Your choices may include a rollover to a new employer's plan, or to a rollover IRA which may be invested in variable or fixed annuities, or other investments such as mutual funds.

WHAT THEY OFFER

With any of these choices you preserve the tax-deferred status of your account and let your total assets continue to compound. There are also some additional benefits, and at least one drawback to each alternative.

PLAN A
TAX-DEFERRED

New employer's plan

+ You begin the new plan with an established base, providing a head start on building a substantial account

+ Fees on employer plans are often smaller than fees for other accounts

− You are limited to investments offered through the plan

Individual Retirement Account

+ You can choose the financial institution that becomes the trustee of your account

+ You can invest your money almost any way you choose, including individual stocks and bonds, mutual funds, or annuities

− You have to create your own income program

Individual Retirement Annuity

+ You can select from a range of providers, choosing a contract that offers the combination of investment portfolios and rate of return you're looking for

+ You can take advantage of the broadest range of withdrawal opportunities, including annuitization

+ With a variable annuity, your beneficiaries are guaranteed your premium and often earnings, which have been periodically locked in, if you should die before beginning to take income

+ With a fixed or variable annuity, you can choose to receive a guaranteed income you can't outlive

− Your fees may be higher than with other options

WHEN CAN YOU DO A ROLLOVER?

You can generally do a qualified rollover from your retirement plan when there's a change in your employment status or your private life. For example:

● **You get a new job, with a new employer**
● **You're let go**
● **You quit or retire**
● **You receive payment from an eligible plan that has ended**
● **Your spouse dies and you get a payout from his or her employer**
● **You get money from a qualified plan as part of a divorce settlement**

PLAN B
STILL
TAX-DEFERRED

DON'T MIX YOUR ACCOUNTS

You have to be careful to maintain a separate investment account for any retirement funds you roll over. If you deposit rollover money into an existing IRA, you may create confusion about taxes you'll owe, especially if money already in the account wasn't tax deductible. Once the two are mingled, you won't be able to separate them again. This may become important when you begin to withdraw your money.

DO IT DIRECTLY

If you roll over retirement money directly from one qualified investment to another, it's a tax-free transaction, and the entire amount goes on growing tax-deferred. But if the payout goes to you first, 20% is automatically withheld, even if you deposit the check immediately in the rollover account.

You'll eventually get the 20% back as long as you deposit the entire amount of the payout within 60 days. But you'll have to wait for the refund until you've filed your income tax return for the year.

The problem may be coming up with the missing 20% in order to make the full deposit. If you don't, the tax law treats that amount as a withdrawal, so you'll owe tax on it and maybe a penalty. What's more, once you've taken a distribution and paid tax on it, that money can never be rolled into another qualified plan. Its tax-deferred status is lost forever.

CHOOSING AN ANNUITY

By rolling over your retirement assets into an annuity, you can choose among various income options, like those that guarantee lifetime income, and not have to worry about orchestrating withdrawals from your savings plans.

INDIRECT ROLLOVER
20% TAX WITHHELD

1035 EXCHANGES

You can exchange one nonqualified annuity for another without owing tax on your earnings following provisions of Internal Revenue Code section 1035, which is why they're known as 1035 exchanges.

But if you surrender one annuity and actually receive the money, which you then use to buy another annuity, that doesn't count as an exchange and you'll be stuck with the tax bill. You can get around that by having

the annuity provider assign, or transfer, the contract directly to another provider.

This rule lets you exchange a fixed annuity for a variable, a variable for a fixed, one variable for another, or make a number of other switches. One thing you can't do is exchange your annuity for a life insurance policy. That's because at your death the insurance policy would allow your beneficiaries to avoid taxes on the amount they received— something annuities don't let them do.

Annuity Income

Annuities exist to provide income in retirement.

You can get annuity income in two ways. You can purchase a **deferred annuity**, typically while you are still working, as a way to help you save for retirement. You determine the amount and frequency of your premiums and when the income will begin, typically in retirement.

Or, you can purchase an **immediate annuity** with a single premium, such as a lump sum payment from a retirement savings plan or the profits from selling your business. As the name implies, immediate annuities begin paying income soon after you purchase the contract.

GROWING MORE FLEXIBLE

The earliest deferred variable annuities offered two choices when you were ready to start receiving income. You could convert your contract to the payout phase, a process called **annuitization**. However, these early variable annuities generally provided income for as long as you lived but left nothing for your beneficiaries when you died. Or, rather than annuitizing, you could surrender your contract, which meant getting your premiums and earnings back in a lump sum, minus expenses, and owing tax on the earnings. But once you chose, you couldn't change your mind.

Since then, many different annuity payout options have been added that offer the appeal of liquidity and flexibility, even though the basic purpose continues to be to provide retirement income. These payout options are also available with immediate annuities if you want to start receiving income right away.

For example, many annuity policies now allow you to take a life annuity with a period certain that guarantees payments until the end of the period even if you die before then. And many contracts offer income that continues for a fixed period, rather than as long as you live. Contracts may also be **commutable** under certain circumstances. That means you can withdraw a lump sum amount after annuitization begins rather than continue to receive regular payments. Though changing your mind may be possible only with certain types of payout plans, the flexibility has real advantages if your life situation changes.

Income Choices

When you're ready to take income, annuity contracts typically offer a number of choices:

- **Lifetime income**
- **Income for a fixed period**
- **Systematic withdrawals**
- **Lump sum withdrawals**

FIGHTING INFLATION

Inflation isn't a new topic, and it certainly isn't a pleasant one. If you're living on $50,000 this year, twenty four years from now it will cost you $100,000 to live the same way, assuming that the inflation rate stays at its current 3%. If the rate goes up, the cost of living will double even more quickly.

There are two ways to handle the effects of inflation: You can live a less comfortable lifestyle or generate additional income. Once you stop working the only way to increase your income is to draw from financial products that can grow faster than the rate of inflation.

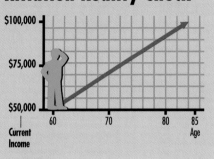

Inflation Reality Check

$100,000

$75,000

$50,000

Current
Income

60   70   80   85
Age

USING VARIABLE ANNUITIES

Having variable annuity income to supplement the money you need in retirement can help make long-term planning easier. Even though the amount of each payment may fluctuate, you can count on receiving income consistently.

Perhaps more important, though, is that you can choose an option that will guarantee income for as long as you live.

And, with a variable annuity, you can spread your money around in a number of investment portfolios. That protects you from having all your eggs in one basket, yet lets you share the benefit when investments in those portfolios grow in value or produce strong earnings, or both.

Making Your Money Last

One of the biggest challenges you'll face in retirement is managing your money so that it will last for the rest of your life. Here are some questions to consider as you make your plans:

1. What effect will taking money out of your various retirement accounts have on their continued ability to grow and provide income for as long as you live?

2. What part of your income can you count on and what part is less predictable?

3. How diversified are your income sources? Are you too vulnerable to major changes in the economy, including declining interest rates?

Immediate Annuity Income

There's nothing like an instant return to provide a sense of security.

Immediate annuities offer something no other retirement plans do: the opportunity to start getting income right away. That's why they're sometimes described as payout annuities.

Since you buy an immediate annuity by paying a single premium, this type of annuity can be a smart choice if you get a one-time pension payout, sell a business, inherit money, or receive an insurance benefit and want to convert these assets to a source of regular future income.

What's more, you can purchase an immediate annuity and convert your cash to income at a time that suits you. Typically, you can buy a contract as late as age 90.

LOOKING AT THE BENEFITS

You can set up your immediate annuity to receive income monthly, quarterly, semi-annually or annually. That can be a big advantage over other income-producing investments such as bonds, which typically pay on a fixed, semi-annual schedule.

And remember that immediate annuities provide an additional benefit, since part of each income payment is return of principal on which you owe no tax.

One criticism sometimes levelled at fixed immediate annuities (and annuities in general) is that you lose access to and control over your assets. However, some immediate annuities let you commute your contract, which means you can take some or all of the cash value minus expenses in a lump sum at any point.

There are even some newer immediate annuities that let you commute your contract even if you've chosen lifetime annuity payments.

FIXED INCOME

A **fixed immediate annuity** provides a steady, reliable stream of income for your lifetime, for two lifetimes (usually yours and your spouse's) or for a certain period of time.

As with other annuities, the amount you get depends on the size of the premium, your age (or joint ages), the interest rate, and the number of guarantees that are provided. For example, a payout guaranteed to last as long as you and your spouse are alive will provide a smaller payment than one based solely on your life.

One issue with this type of annuity is that the fixed income is vulnerable to inflation, since the cost of living will most likely increase over your lifetime but the money you get from the annuity will not.

For some people, though, being assured that a specific amount will arrive on a regular basis is more appealing than having to take responsibility for allocating assets or worry about getting smaller payments in some periods. For example, a surviving spouse who inherits a substantial sum can avoid having to make investment decisions by converting the money to steady annuity income.

Fixed immediate annuities might also be appropriate for older people. The older you are when the annuity begins, the higher the payment amount. That's because more of the principal is repaid each time.

WHERE THE MONEY GOES

When an annuitant dies sooner than expected, what happens to the assets that have accumulated in the annuity contract? If the payout is for a term certain, the beneficiary continues to receive income for that period. If it is a lifetime payout, the assets revert to the issuing company, where they are used to provide income payments to other annuitants who live longer than expected. In fact, the guarantee of lifetime income based on average life expectancy assumes that just as some people will live longer, others will die sooner.

VARIABLE INCOME

Variable immediate annuities combine the assurance of regular income with the advantage of continuing participation in equity markets through the investment portfolios offered through the contract.

That means the amount of income you receive can increase over time, so that you're in a better position to keep pace with or exceed the rate of inflation.

Of course the amount you receive can also decrease at any time if investment performance declines. Historically, however, the equity markets have been a good way to beat inflation over the long haul.

If you have a long retirement, your investment choices will have an extended period in which to grow and produce income. Most variable immediate annuities offer the same types and varieties of investment accounts that deferred contracts provide. Most also allow you to choose the benchmark rate by which your portfolio's performance will be measured.

In an immediate annuity, the death benefit protection is in the form of continuing payments to your beneficiaries for a specified number of years or a cash refund of the unpaid contract value remaining at your death. These assurances offset the concern that the issuing company might not pay out all you have invested if you die sooner than you expected.

WHERE ANNUITIES FIT

Most experts suggest that an immediate fixed or variable annuity works best as part of a package that includes income from Social Security, your qualified retirement plans, IRAs, and your other investments. Although you should never count on just a single source of income, they suggest that annuity income can be an important part of your total retirement income package, providing a stream of income that you cannot outlive.

Lifetime Income

Being confident of your income can make retirement easier.

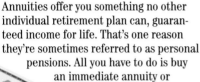

Annuities offer you something no other individual retirement plan can, guaranteed income for life. That's one reason they're sometimes referred to as personal pensions. All you have to do is buy an immediate annuity or **annuitize** your deferred annuity, and choose one of the lifetime payout plans offered by your annuity contract. What's more, you can choose a variable payout that will increase your income over time, provided the value of your investment portfolios continues to grow.

As an added plus, each annuitized payment in a nonqualified contract is partially tax free, since you're getting back some of your principal each time. That means you'll have a larger amount to spend than if your payments were fully taxable.

With a deferred annuity the income you receive when you first annuitize is produced by the assets in your annuity, also known as its **contract value**. That includes the premiums you've paid and what you've earned during the accumulation period. If you buy an immediate annuity, there is no accumulation period and the initial payment is based on the premium.

ALL IN THE TIMING

When you're ready to start receiving income from a deferred annuity, all you have to do is ask. You let the annuity company know that you want to convert your contract from accumulation to payout, which is called **annuitizing your contract**. You'll have to indicate the payout option you've chosen, whether you want a fixed or variable stream of income (or some of each), and the date you want to receive the first income payment.

If you have a tax-deferred annuity (TDA), an annuity in a qualified retirement plan, or an annuity in an IRA, the federal government requires you to start taking income by April 1 of the year after you turn 70½.

SET THE TIME

Your nonqualified deferred annuity contract will stipulate a maturity date by which you must begin collecting income. Typically it's in the year you reach the age set either by the state in which you live or by the company issuing the policy. Generally it's 85 or older though in some states, it's currently 90. But maturity dates are rarely an issue, since there are usually good reasons to start income payments earlier.

With nonqualified plans, you have much more flexibility over when to start. You can make the choice at almost any time while the contract is in effect—for example, as early as age 45, at the time you retire, or later. The only deadlines are those imposed by state law or the terms of your contract.

Income Choices

The income you get from your annuity depends on a number of factors. The most important are the premium or purchase payment (for immediate annuities) or the total accumulated value of the contract (for deferred annuities), your age when you begin taking annuity payments, the payout option you choose, and whether the income is fixed or variable.

FIXED

If you have a **fixed annuity**, the payout amount is traditionally fixed. For example, if you receive $500 in your first payment, you'll get $500 in your last one—and every payment in between. Some newer contracts, though, build in the potential for periodic increases of 1%, 2%, or 3% to account for increases in the cost of living.

FIXED

VARIABLE

VARIABLE

If you have a **variable annuity**, you can choose the way your income amount will be figured. You can generally select variable income, which fluctuates depending on the performance of your investment portfolios. Or, with many contracts, you can also choose fixed income or a combination of fixed and variable income to provide both stability and the potential for growth.

CHOOSING FIXED INCOME

The appeal of choosing fixed income is that you know exactly how much you'll be getting, and the payment is guaranteed. For people concerned about decreasing payments, that can be a comforting thought. On the other hand, the income amount won't increase either, which means your buying power will shrink as a result of inflation.

Another appealing feature of fixed income may be that it's easy to understand how the amount you're receiving is calculated. It is based on:

- The dollar value of the contract when income payments start
- Interest earnings guaranteed in the contract
- Annuity tables that project your life expectancy based on your age

As a rule of thumb, the larger your contract value and the older you are when you begin to receive income, the larger each payment will be.

CHOOSING GROWTH

If you choose variable, or combined fixed and variable income, you're taking the risk that the amount of income you receive in any payment can be less than in the previous one if the value of the investment portfolios you have chosen declines. But many experts agree that the risk is offset by the likelihood that over time equity investments will increase rather than decrease in value. That growth potential is the reason why a variable payout gives you the opportunity for increasing income in the future and the ability to offset the impact of inflation. It's also one of the reasons you chose a variable annuity to accumulate assets.

The amount you receive in each payment will reflect the performance of your investment portfolios. If your investment return after expenses is greater than the benchmark growth rate—called the **assumed interest rate (AIR)**—that is in effect with your contract, your payment will increase. If your return is less than the AIR, your payment will decrease. With many contracts you are asked to choose between two or more benchmark growth rates, 3% and 6%, for example, or 3.5% and 5%. With other contracts, the benchmark is set either by the contract issuer or by state law. (There's more about how AIRs work on pages 88 and 104.)

Payout Options

You can take annuity income in the way that suits you best.

When you buy an immediate annuity, or when you're ready to convert your deferred annuity into income, you will have to choose the way in which that income will be paid. Every contract offers a range of choices that provide different benefits and different amounts of income, and cover different periods of time.

WHAT YOUR OPTIONS ARE

While some contracts offer more income options than others, or use different language to describe your choices, you generally have six or seven alternatives, each with distinctive characteristics. You can get a good sense of how they differ by analyzing the information in the chart.

Payout option	How payout amount is determined
LIFE ANNUITY	Based on contract value, your age when payments begin, and interest rate (if fixed income) or investment experience and AIR (if variable income)
LIFE INCOME WITH PERIOD, OR TERM, CERTAIN	Based on contract value, your age when payments begin, interest rate (if fixed income) or investment experience and AIR (if variable income), and the length of the guarantee (typically from 5 to 20 years)
LIFE INCOME WITH REFUND PAYOUT	Based on contract value, your age when payments begin, interest rate (if fixed income) or investment experience and AIR (if variable income), and the refund guarantee
JOINT AND SURVIVOR LIFE ANNUITY	Based on contract value, your age and the age of your joint annuitant when payments begin, and interest rate (if fixed income) or investment experience and AIR (if variable income)
JOINT AND SURVIVOR ANNUITY WITH PERIOD CERTAIN	Based on contract value, your age and the age of your joint annuitant when payments begin, interest rate (if fixed income) or investment experience and AIR (if variable income), and the length of the guarantee (typically from 5 to 20 years)
FIXED AMOUNT (AVAILABLE ONLY WITH A FIXED INCOME PAYOUT)	You say how much income you want
FIXED PERIOD	Payment amount is determined by the length of time you choose to receive income, the contract value, interest rate (if fixed income) or investment experience and AIR (if variable income)

ANNUITIES AT A GLANCE

Variable annuities were introduced in 1952—as the College Retirement Equity Fund (CREF) by the Teacher's Insurance and Annuity Association (TIAA)—to provide the twin benefits of lifetime income and the inflation-beating power of equity investments.

Though there have been enormous changes in variable annuities since they first appeared—including how readily available these long-term plans have become—their underlying purpose hasn't changed: It's still to provide a source of lifetime income that can outrun the eroding effects of inflation.

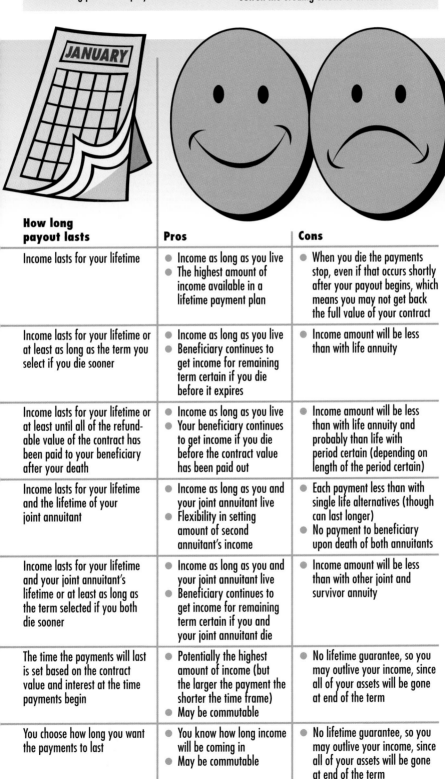

How long payout lasts	Pros	Cons
Income lasts for your lifetime	• Income as long as you live • The highest amount of income available in a lifetime payment plan	• When you die the payments stop, even if that occurs shortly after your payout begins, which means you may not get back the full value of your contract
Income lasts for your lifetime or at least as long as the term you select if you die sooner	• Income as long as you live • Beneficiary continues to get income for remaining term certain if you die before it expires	• Income amount will be less than with life annuity
Income lasts for your lifetime or at least until all of the refundable value of the contract has been paid to your beneficiary after your death	• Income as long as you live • Your beneficiary continues to get income if you die before the contract value has been paid out	• Income amount will be less than with life annuity and probably than life with period certain (depending on length of the period certain)
Income lasts for your lifetime and the lifetime of your joint annuitant	• Income as long as you and your joint annuitant live • Flexibility in setting amount of second annuitant's income	• Each payment less than with single life alternatives (though can last longer) • No payment to beneficiary upon death of both annuitants
Income lasts for your lifetime and your joint annuitant's lifetime or at least as long as the term selected if you both die sooner	• Income as long as you and your joint annuitant live • Beneficiary continues to get income for remaining term certain if you and your joint annuitant die	• Income amount will be less than with other joint and survivor annuity
The time the payments will last is set based on the contract value and interest at the time payments begin	• Potentially the highest amount of income (but the larger the payment the shorter the time frame) • May be commutable	• No lifetime guarantee, so you may outlive your income, since all of your assets will be gone at end of the term
You choose how long you want the payments to last	• You know how long income will be coming in • May be commutable	• No lifetime guarantee, so you may outlive your income, since all of your assets will be gone at end of the term

Annuitization Strategy

You can control the flow of retirement income.

If using annuity payments to provide income is the strategy that seems to make the most sense, you can select a payout plan that suits your individual situation. All nonqualified annuity contracts offer some tax-free income until the total amount of your premium has been repaid. All but two of them promise income for life. You can find a summary of their features on pages 100-101.

INFLUENCING

There are several key factors to consider when you weigh the various payout options. It makes sense to review them with your financial advisor before making up your mind.

Who will get the money?

JOINT AND SURVIVOR OR SINGLE LIFE

Should the payout be life only or joint and survivor? For many people, wanting to provide lifelong income for a spouse or other beneficiary is the driving force in choosing a joint and survivor payout. Each individual payment amount is less than with a single life annuity, but the total over two lifetimes can be more, sometimes much more.

When isn't a joint and survivor policy the wiser decision? Among the factors to consider are how much income each of you has from other sources and how healthy you are. For example, if you own an annuity and your spouse has a good defined benefit plan, taking a single life annuity might make sense. It would provide more income than a joint and survivor payout and your spouse is already guaranteed lifetime income. Similarly, if your spouse is ill, and unlikely to outlive you, a single life annuity might be the wiser choice.

What percentage should the survivor get?

50% OR 100%

What percent of income should the survivor receive? The follow-up decision is what percentage of the income that you receive while you're both alive should be paid to the surviving partner. There are usually several choices, with the least being 50% and the most 100%.

The decision involves trade-offs, as so many things do. If the surviving partner gets 100% of the income, the amount you get while you are both alive will be less. But the goal in choosing that alternative is that the survivor will have as much income as he or she needs.

On the other hand, a variable annuity paying the survivor 50% may provide sufficient income, since the living expenses of one person should be less than for two. Additionally, the variable annuity paying the survivor 50% can actually provide enough growth to make up the difference over time if the investment portfolios you've chosen produce strong returns.

In one recent example, a surviving spouse received an initial 50% payment of $228 following the annuitant's death. Three years later, the amount had climbed back to $414, only $42 less than they had been receiving together. Of course, there is the potential for payments to decrease if the investment portfolios you've chosen do not produce strong returns.

THE FIXED ALTERNATIVE

There are circumstances when knowing exactly what you can count on each month may seem more appealing than the potential for growth.

You can get fixed income from your variable annuity by using either part or all of the accumulated value of your contract. The way it works is that the assets in your investment accounts are liquidated and deposited into the annuity provider's general account. The company then takes on the responsibility for making regular income payments.

With some contracts, you may also be able to choose a fixed payout that increases in increments of 1%, 2%, or 3%, reflecting increases in the cost of living. With this feature, your payments may initially be smaller than if you had not chosen increasing payments.

F A C T O R S

How long will you get the money?

PERIOD CERTAIN OR FIXED TERM

Should you choose a life annuity that guarantees a certain number of payments? One reason people give for choosing not to annuitize is that they're afraid if they die shortly after they begin receiving payments, they will forfeit a large portion of the amount they spent to purchase the annuity. To avoid that situation, some people choose a period certain payout guaranteeing that they or their beneficiaries will receive income for at least a minimum period, typically 5, 10 or 20 years.

You can choose a period certain payout whether you take a single life or joint and survivor option. Although the guarantee reduces the amount you get somewhat, most experts agree it's a smart choice.

Should you take a payout that doesn't guarantee life income? If the reason you're annuitizing is being able to count on income for as long as you live, you should choose the lifetime guarantee. But there are situations when getting a larger amount of money each month or insuring payments will last a specific amount of time is a smart decision.

Some appealing features are that these payout models can produce the largest income payments in the short term. Also, when you select this option, you typically have the opportunity to **commute**, or cash in, your annuity for a lump sum rather than receive income payments in the future. In addition, in these plans part of your income payment is always tax free. With life payouts, you may end up owing tax on the entire income amount of each payout if you live long enough to have gotten your entire cost basis back. Of course, this is not really a negative since it means that you're getting back more than you put in.

NOW AND LATER
What if you want to receive income payments while you continue to build your retirement assets?
A **split-funded annuity** lets you begin receiving income from a portion of your premium immediately, while the rest of the money goes into a deferred annuity. The advantage is that you can get some income right away, while the balance compounds tax-deferred, building up your asset value to provide even more income in the future when you begin to take income from the deferred portion as well.

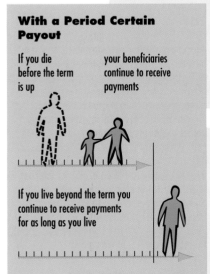

With a Period Certain Payout

If you die before the term is up — your beneficiaries continue to receive payments

If you live beyond the term you continue to receive payments for as long as you live

Understanding Variable Income

Variable income means the amount of your payments will change to reflect investment performance.

The point of choosing variable income is that if the value of the investment portfolios you have chosen in your annuity contract continues to grow during the payout period, the amount of income you receive can go up as well.

Of course, there's no way to project future performance, and your income could go down as well as up, especially in the short term. But between 1952 when variable annuities were introduced and 2001, large-company stocks provided positive returns in 38 years and negative returns in only 12 years, according to Ibbotson Associates.

CHOOSING A RATE

As part of selecting a variable payout, you must generally choose among two or more assumed interest rates, or AIRs. That's a benchmark against which your actual investment performance will be compared after your income payments begin. Typically, companies offer AIRs that vary between one and a half and three percentage points. For example, AIRs of 3.5% and 5% may be offered by one annuity company, and AIRs of 3% and 6% by another.

If you choose the lower rate, you get a smaller initial income payment than you would with a higher rate. But the performance of your investment portfolios can meet or exceed the benchmark you've set more easily than if the AIR were higher. Each time performance minus expenses exceeds the benchmark, your income increases. That can translate into more rapid income growth, and eventually into larger payout amounts.

For example, if you choose a rate of 3% and the actual net gain in the value of your investment portfolios is five percentage points, your income will increase. But if you've chosen a 6% rate and the net gain is five percentage points, your income will decline even though there has been growth.

ACCUMULATION PERIOD

Invested monthly	**$500**
Value of account at time of annuitization	**$100,000**

WHEN YOU ANNUITIZE

1. Account value is fixed in time at $100,000

2. Your present age and the AIR benchmark you've chosen determine how much per $1,000 in your account will be in your first payment

3. Number of thousands in account
Rate

	100
	x $5.94

Your first monthly payment = **$594.00**

Rates for a Variable Annuity with Assumed Net Return Rate of

3.5% (AIR)

Amount of first monthly payment for each $1,000 after fees

Age of Annuitant	Amount per $1,000
63	5.63
64	5.78
65	5.94
66	6.11
67	6.29
68	

FINDING THE INITIAL PAYMENT

Once the benchmark has been set, you can compute the minimum amount you'll receive in your first payment by using the tables included in your contract. There's a different table for each of the AIRs and payment options the contract offers.

For example, assume you owned a variable annuity contract whose payment tables showed that a life annuity with an AIR of 3.5% would pay $5.94 for each $1,000 of accumulated contract value if you annuitized at age 65. If your contract was worth $100,000, your first monthly check (or direct deposit) would be $594 ($5.94 times 100, the number of $1,000s in $100,000).

ADDED APPEAL

Choosing variable lifetime income has a major advantage. In addition to money coming in on a regular basis, the income payments you receive can increase over time. In any period when equity investments are performing well—or what's known as a bull market—the amount you receive will tend to increase.

Once the amount you're receiving increases, any decreases in value are based on the most recent payments, not the amount of your first payment. For example, if over three years the amount you received increased from $594 to $785 and then values declined for a time, your payments might go down to $735 or even $675. It is less likely, based on historical figures, that your payment amount will drop below $594, though in a serious downturn, or in a downturn occurring soon after your income stream began, it could.

Annuity History   3.5% Assumed Interest Rate

This example demonstrates that the income you receive with a variable payout can move up or down from period to period. The example shows past performance, but doesn't predict what might happen in the future, which depends on the combined performance of your individual portfolios.

Date	Payment	Date	Payment	Date	Payment
Jul. 1993	$267.32	Jan. 1997	$392.82	Jul. 1999	$435.13
Oct. 1993	266.12	Apr. 1997	380.33	Oct. 1999	468.58
Jan. 1994	268.20	Jul. 1997	379.37	Jan. 2000	485.70
Apr. 1994	283.86	Oct. 1997	388.86	Apr. 2000	490.45
Jul. 1994	300.70	Jan. 1998	399.97	Jul. 2000	480.28
Oct. 1994	323.36	Apr. 1998	403.59	Oct. 2000	482.61
Jan. 1995					76
Apr. 1995					
Jul. 1995					
Oct. 1995					
Jan. 1996					
Apr. 1996					
Jul. 1996	364.42	Apr. 1999	403.20		

When the value of an annuity unit in your account goes up, your monthly payment increases. When the value decreases, the amount goes down for that period, but can go up again.

HOW VARIABLE INCOME WORKS

After the first payout, the amount you receive can go up or down depending on the performance of your investment portfolios. The first step in the process is to convert your first payment into a set number of annuity units. This is done by dividing the initial payment by the annuity unit value at the time of the payment. Then, this constant number of units is multiplied by the annuity unit value at the time of each future payment to determine the amount of that payout in dollars. Here's how it works:

STEP ONE: DETERMINING ANNUITY UNITS

In the example above, the first payment was $594. If the annuity unit value at the time of the payment was $10, you would be credited with 59.4 units (594 ÷ 10 = 59.4). The number of annuity units is then fixed so you always have the same number of annuity units as long as you continue to receive income.

STEP TWO: ASSESSING PORTFOLIO PERFORMANCE

Next, the company determines the value of an annuity unit for your next payment, which can increase or decrease based on the performance of your investment portfolios. If the net return on your investment portfolios is greater than the benchmark you have chosen, the value of the annuity unit increases. If the net return is less than the benchmark, the value declines. For example, if the annual net return on your investment portfolio results in a 6.3% increase over the benchmark, the unit value would increase to $10.63 ($10 x 1.063).

STEP THREE: CALCULATING NEW INCOME AMOUNT

Finally, the company multiplies the new unit value times the number of annuity units to arrive at the amount of your payment. In this example, the new monthly payment after one year would be $631.42 (59.4 x $10.63 = $631.42). Of course, the amount could go down as well as up in any given period.

Reading Your Statement

You'll get regular reports on your annuity's performance.

Whether your variable annuity contract is accumulating value or you've begun to receive income, you can stay up to date on where you stand, thanks to the statements you get regularly from your annuity provider. Though your statement won't look exactly like the sample that's shown here, it should provide the basic information you need.

If you want to track the way your investment portfolios are performing in relation to portfolios with similar objectives that are also available in the contract, you'll have current numbers. You may decide, for example, based on those figures, to transfer assets from one portfolio to another. Or you may decide to reassess your overall allocation.

Your annual contract summary recaps the beginning value plus additional payments and the ending (or current) value for a contract that is still in the accumulation phase. The difference between what you've paid and the current value is the growth, or change in investment value. In this example, that's $63,217.22 over an eight-year period, or a $7,902.15 annualized return.

In addition, the statement covers the most recent period's change in investment value, as well as that information for each of your investment portfolios.

After you begin to receive income from a variable annuity, your monthly statement will detail the total value of your current income payment, along with the federal and state taxes being withheld. This statement also provides a year to date summary of the taxable and non-taxable amounts of income you've received from your annuity.

If you choose to have your income direct deposited, the company will handle that transaction, or it will mail you a check for the current amount.

Annual Contract Summary

Contract Summary

	Since inception 04/17 to 04/17
Beginning Value	$25,180.59
Additional Purchases	5,500.00
Change in investment Value	63,217.22
Ending Value as of 04/17	**$93,897.81**

Investment Options Summary

Beginning of Period January 17

Investment Options	Number of Units	Value per Unit	Total Value
Portfolio I	1,202.461	39,292.813	$47,248.08
Portfolio II	526.816	43,331.280	22,827.61
Portfolio III	528.036	23,817.695	12,576.60
Total Value			**$82,652.29**

The investment options summary provides up-to-date information on the investment portfolios you've selected from among those offered in your annuity contract and helps explain the numbers in the contract summary.

The number of units shows the way you have allocated your money. In this case, you have more than half your assets in Portfolio I, and the balance split between Portfolios II and III.

The income payment you receive each month is based on the number of income, or annuity, units you own in each of your investment portfolios multiplied by the value per income unit. Here, for example, the 80.383 units in Portfolio A times a value of $1.832836 produces income of $147.33.

The number of units remains fixed, but the value of each unit typically increases or decreases regularly, though the amount of change is not predictable. In this example, the smaller number of units in Portfolio A produces slightly more income than Portfolio B because the unit value is greater.

Monthly Statement

Income Payment

	Number of Income Units	Value per Income Unit	Income Amount
Portfolio A	+80.383	1.832836	$147.33
Portfolio B	+110.290	1.332219	$146.93
The total value of your income payment			$294.26
Federal Taxes Withheld			-100.00
State Taxes Withheld			-9.45
Income Net of Taxes			184.81

The above amount will be deposited into your account

Year to Date Income

	Income Amount
Taxable Income	1,045.41
Non-Taxable Income	948.50
Year to Date Income	$1,993.91
Federal Tax Withheld	-400.00
State Tax Withheld	-62.20
Year to Date Income Net of Taxes	$1,531.71

This Period 01/17 to 04/17
$82,652.29
0.00
11,245.52
$93,897.81

When you annuitize a non-qualified annuity, a portion of each annuity payment is generally not taxed. That amount represents the return of your principal. In this example, 48% of your total $1,993.91 year to date income is not taxable, substantially boosting the amount you have to spend.

But, if you choose a life-time income option, when all of the principal has been re-paid to you, which typically occurs if you live longer than your life expectancy deter-mined at the time you annuitized, all of your subse-quent income will be from earnings and will be taxable.

End of Period April 17		
Number of Units	Value per Unit	Total Value
1,202.461	44,489.349	$53,496.71
526.816	49,058.059	25,844.59
528.036	27,567.271	14,556.51
		$93,897.61

The value per unit, which is different for each portfolio, changes to reflect the perfor-mance of a portfolio's underlying investments. For example, the nearly equal number of units in Portfolios II and III have very different unit values, so those portfolios have different total values.

However, all the unit values have increased in this example, boosting the total value of your contract to $93,897.61.

Taxing Annuity Income

The way you receive annuity income determines
the tax you pay.

When you put money into a tax-deferred retirement plan, you postpone paying tax on your earnings until you begin getting income from your account. There's little debate about the advantages that tax deferral provides: It's one of the reasons to buy a nonqualified annuity. What can be confusing, however, is what taxes you do owe and when you owe them.

TAXES ON ANNUITY INCOME

If you annuitize a nonqualified annuity, part of the income you receive is the return of your **cost basis**, or premium. The rest comes from your accumulated earnings. The portion that represents a return of your premium is tax free because you paid tax on that money before you bought your annuity. The balance, however, which is your earnings on the premium, is taxable.

If you receive periodic or systematic payments or make occasional withdrawals from your nonqualified deferred annuity during the accumulation phase, the tax law assumes you don't begin to get your premium back until you have received all of the earnings. That means all of your income is taxable in the early years of periodic withdrawals. In addition to the income tax, you may owe an additional 10% penalty if you're younger than 59½.

If you take a lump sum, you owe tax plus the potential penalty on all of the earnings in the year you make the withdrawal.

With a qualified plan or TDA, the total amount of each income payment you receive is generally taxable because you reduced your salary by the amount of the premium and paid less in taxes at the time you purchased or added to the contract. The same is true of an annuity you own in an IRA if you were entitled to a tax deduction for your contribution.

> **TAXING FACT**
> When you estimate the income you need in retirement, don't forget that you'll still owe income taxes.

FINDING WHAT YOU OWE

When you receive annuity payments, you find the taxable portion of each payment by using an **exclusion ratio**.

FIXED ANNUITIES

With a fixed annuity, you divide the premiums paid for the annuity by the expected return, determined by IRS tables. The resulting fraction or percentage is the nontaxable portion of each payment until all of the investment amount has been returned. The balance is taxable.

$$\frac{\text{Premiums paid (Cost basis)}}{\text{Expected return}} = \begin{array}{l}\textbf{Nontaxable}\\ \textbf{portion of}\\ \textbf{payments}\end{array}$$

for example

For example, if you invested $100,000 in an annuity, and the expected total return is $250,000 based on your life expectancy and the interest rate being paid, you'd divide the investment total by the expected return:

$$\frac{\$100,000}{\$250,000} = \textbf{40\%} \begin{array}{l}\textbf{Nontaxable}\\ \textbf{portion of}\\ \textbf{payments}\end{array}$$

That means that 40% of the payments you receive in that year are free of tax, and 60% are taxed at your regular rate. So if you were getting $650 a month, you'd owe tax on $390 of it, or on $4,680 of your $7,800 annual income.

Monthly income	$	650
Percentage taxable	x	.60
Taxable income	= $	390
	x	12
Annual taxable income	= $	4,680

WHAT YOU PAY TAXES ON

	Nonqualified Annuities		Qualified Annuities
Payout	Cost Basis	Earnings	Cost Basis + Earnings
Annuitize	NO TAX	TAX	TAX
Periodic	NO TAX	TAX	TAX
Lump sum	NO TAX	TAX	TAX

VARIABLE ANNUITIES

With a variable annuity, the excluded amount is figured a little differently, since there is no way to predict the expected total return. Here, you divide your cost basis, or the amount you spent on premiums, by the number of years you expect payments to be made. In a fixed term contract, the number of years is the same as the fixed term. When you arrange for lifetime payment, you use your life expectancy depending on the payout option you choose to determine the number of years.

$$\frac{\text{Cost basis}}{\text{Number of years of expected payments}} = \begin{array}{l}\textbf{Nontaxable}\\ \textbf{portion of}\\ \textbf{annual income}\end{array}$$

for example

For example, if you had paid in $100,000 and your life expectancy was 20 years at the time you annuitized, the annual income you could exclude from taxes would be $5,000.

$$\frac{\$100,000}{20} = \textbf{\$5,000} \begin{array}{l}\textbf{Nontaxable}\\ \textbf{portion of}\\ \textbf{annual income}\end{array}$$

In this case, after you collected payments for 20 years, all of your income would become taxable.

BENEFICIARY TAXES

If you've started to collect income from your annuity, but die before all of the amount you're guaranteed has been paid, your beneficiary gets the remaining income. Those payments are free of income tax to the same extent they were free of income tax during your lifetime, and this continues until the value of the cost basis has been fully repaid. The remaining income is fully taxable.

If you die before you annuitize, your beneficiary gets the death benefit provided in the contract. The cost basis is returned tax free, and the balance is taxed in the manner which reflects the way it's received: lump sum, periodic payments within five years, or annuitization starting within one year after the date of your death. The payout method is determined by the terms of the contract and who the beneficiary is.

PREMATURE DISTRIBUTIONS

One of the limitations of tax-deferred investing is the 10% penalty on the taxable portion of withdrawals you make before you reach age 59½. Congress imposes this penalty to discourage you from touching your retirement money before you actually retire.

There are some exceptions for withdrawing from deferred annuities without federal tax penalty, though you do pay income tax on the taxable amount:

- You can withdraw if you are disabled
- You can annuuitize for your life or joint lifetime, or set up a series of substantially equal periodic payments to last for your lifetime or the joint lifetimes of you and your spouse
- In certain circumstances with a qualified annuity contract, you can use a portion of your contract value to pay higher education expenses or buy a first home

The penalty doesn't apply to immediate annuity payments, which you can begin to receive at any age.

PAYING ESTIMATED TAXES

While you work, your employer typically withholds enough from your paycheck to cover the income taxes you owe. After you retire, however, it's your job to figure out— and prepay—the correct amount.

If you expect to owe at least $1,000, you must make quarterly estimated tax payments. Although annuity companies will withhold taxes from your income payments, you'll have to coordinate with the company to determine what you owe and to be sure the paperwork is in order.

Required Withdrawals

With some plans, you're locked into a withdrawal schedule.

If you have a traditional IRA, you must begin taking income by a set time: April 1 of the year following the year you turn 70½. And you must establish a plan for gradually withdrawing your assets over your lifetime. That's true whether your money is in an annuity, mutual fund or any of the other investments permitted in the plan.

The same requirements apply to 401(k) and 403(b) plans and to qualified individual retirement plans such as Keoghs and Simplified Employee Pensions (SEPs) if you're an owner of the business that set up the plan. (If you're an employee who has a Keogh, 401(k), or SEP but are not an owner, you can postpone withdrawals as long as you continue to work.)

With these retirement plans, you have the benefits of tax-deferred earnings while your contributions accumulate. But Uncle Sam wants to be sure you use these savings for retirement income, not to leave to an estate. That's the reason you have to start taking money out. It's the tradeoff for the privilege of tax deferral.

FIGURING WHAT TO TAKE

"How much do you have?" "How much must you withdraw?"

The mandatory amount you must withdraw after age 70½ is based on the total amount of all your traditional IRA accounts combined. You can take a portion of this amount from various IRA accounts or withdraw the entire amount from a single account.

One benefit of taking it from a single source is that you can protect those accounts that are growing at a faster rate.

HOW TO FIGURE WITHDRAWAL AMOUNTS

The rules for figuring the minimum amount you must withdraw each year after you turn 70½, officially known as your **minimum required distribution (MRD)**, were simplified in 2001, making the calculation much easier.

It's actually just a three-step process:

- You find the value of your account at the end of your plan's fiscal year, usually December 31
- You look up the **uniform withdrawal factor** you must use based on your current age in IRS Publication 590
- You divide your account balance by the uniform withdrawal factor to find your MRD

For example, if you had $300,000 in your IRA on December 31, 2001, and you turned 70½ in 2002, you use 26.2 as the uniform withdrawal factor, or divisor, producing a required withdrawal of $11,450.

IRA assets		$300,000
Withdrawal factor	÷	26.2
MRD		$ 11,450

The next year you follow the same process, dividing your account balance at the end of the previous year by your new uniform withdrawal factor to determine how much you withdraw.

If your account increases in value, as it has the potential to do, you may end up having to withdraw more in the later years of your retirement than in the earlier ones. That's because the uniform withdrawal factor drops each year. For example, when you're 75, it's 21.8 and when you're 85, it's 13.8.

For example, if your account were worth $330,000 when you were 75, you'd have to withdraw $15,138.

IRA assets		$330,000
Withdrawal factor	÷	21.8
MRD		$ 15,138

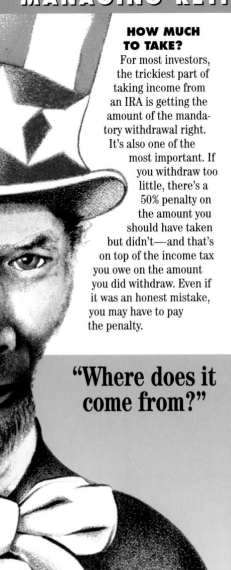

HOW MUCH TO TAKE?

For most investors, the trickiest part of taking income from an IRA is getting the amount of the mandatory withdrawal right. It's also one of the most important. If you withdraw too little, there's a 50% penalty on the amount you should have taken but didn't—and that's on top of the income tax you owe on the amount you did withdraw. Even if it was an honest mistake, you may have to pay the penalty.

One of the advantages of owning an annuity within your IRA is that the annuity company will compute the minimum required distribution you must withdraw and either send you a check or deposit the money in an account you designate. In addition, the annuity can guarantee that your income will last your lifetime. That's one reason people often choose to roll retirement assets over into an annuity before the time for required withdrawals arrives.

STARTING SOONER

You don't have to wait until you reach 70½ to begin taking income. The danger of starting at 59½, though, is that it's possible—even easy—to take more than you planned and risk running out of money down the road unless you are guaranteed lifetime income.

"Where does it come from?"

If your IRA is diversified among a number of different investments, you have to decide which ones to liquidate each year to satisfy the mandatory withdrawal requirements. You could sell stock, but there's no way to be sure you are selling at a time when you'll realize the greatest profit. If you sell a CD, you might have to pay a penalty if you haven't scheduled the maturity date just right. A better approach may be to move assets gradually into a mutual fund from which you can withdraw on a regular basis.

And an even simpler way is to purchase an annuity with your IRA money, which creates a worry-free way to receive the amount that meets the minimum withdrawal requirement.

"When must you start?"

From a tax standpoint, it's generally a good idea to take your first mandatory withdrawal in the same calendar year you turn 70½, rather than waiting until April 1 of the following year. If you wait, you have to make two withdrawals in one year (the first for the year you turned 70½ and the one required for the next year). Because you're taxed on the combined amount of the withdrawals, you run the risk of being bumped into a higher income tax bracket. That would mean paying more tax than you would have by splitting the amount between two years.

You could avoid the complexities of creating a regular schedule of withdrawals by taking all the money out of your IRA in a lump sum. But making this choice means you'll owe tax on the total value of your IRA accounts in a single year, which could mean potentially paying tax at the highest federal rate. It also means you'd lose continuing tax-deferred growth.

TIME TO CHOOSE

Under the new rules, you no longer need to choose your beneficiary by the time you must take your first distribution. Instead, your beneficiary can be named as late as the end of the year following the year you die. The only exception occurs if your spouse is more than ten years younger than you are. Then, if you name him or her before you begin required withdrawals you can use a larger divisor, reducing your required distribution.

Income Strategies

You need a plan to insure your income meets your needs.

Making the leap from deciding to take retirement income to putting that decision into action can be nerve-wracking. That's because the choices you make can mean a major difference in the way you live—sometimes for 30 years or more. And putting off decisions often seems easier than making them. Deep down, lots of people hope that things will just work out.

Realistically, though, you get the best results when you determine the income you'll need, weigh various strategies for providing it, and select the one that promises to best meet your needs.

WHAT THE ISSUES ARE

To make strategic decisions about the best way to use the immediate annuity you have purchased or the assets in your deferred annuity to provide a secure retirement, you need to know:

- Your plans for the money

- The right time to start getting the income

- The tax consequences of various ways of receiving income

Make a Plan

Pick the Right Time

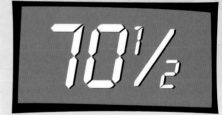

PLANS FOR THE MONEY

In choosing a payout strategy, the way you intend to use the income makes a big impact on your decision.

If you own a deferred annuity and plan to make a large, one-time investment, a lump sum can provide that money.

If you own a deferred annuity and want extra income to supplement your budget or cover extraordinary expenses before you retire, periodic or systematic withdrawals can provide it while giving the balance of your assets more time to grow.

If you're counting on lifetime income to be a part of your regular living-expense budget, pay for the extras that make life fun, or provide a source of cash you can use to create an emergency fund, annuity payments from your immediate annuity or annuitized deferred annuity are designed to provide it.

SETTING THE TIME

If your deferred annuity is part of a qualified plan or an IRA, you generally have to make your choice by the time you reach age 70½. With nonqualified annuities, you've usually got another fifteen years or more before you must make a decision. While there are advantages in that flexibility, the drawback can be a tendency to procrastinate.

You can make an argument for postponing taking income until the last minute, especially if you seem to be managing without it. Then, when you do start, the amount you get will be larger. For example, in some circumstances a person who begins taking income at age 85 might receive almost twice the amount in the initial payment as someone who began at age 62.

But there are often reasons for timing annuity payouts to begin when you retire, or even somewhat earlier. Since juggling various streams of income can be a major challenge, having a period of time to get accustomed to allocating your resources can be smart.

Personalized Plans

Experts say that you may need more income early in your retirement than you will later on. And you may be more comfortable spending money on travel, for example, if you've deliberately created a stream of income designed to pay for it.

To be sure you have the money you want when you want it, you might ask your annuity provider about personalized payout plans or innovative programs for allocating your income. One strategy is to split your variable annuity payout into two streams, one to be paid out over your and your spouse's lifetimes and the other to be paid over five or ten years. For exam-ple, suppose you had a $300,000 annuity and allocated 75% ($225,000) to life income and 25% ($75,000) to a ten-year payout.

The amount you received during the shorter payout—perhaps $8,000 to $9,000 annually—could pay for extended travel or other things you've wanted to do. And since you'd planned the income specifically for that purpose, you could spend it with a clear conscience. At the same time, you'd be guaranteed income for life, based on the balance of the contract value.

CREATING A REVENUE STREAM

If you decide that the promise of income for life and the advantages of a regular return of nontaxable premiums as part of each income payment make sense for you, it's time for the next round of choices. The order in which you deal with them may vary, but these are the things you have to consider:

- Is the growth potential of variable income more important to your long-term plan than the predictability of stable fixed income? Or would you prefer to have some variable income and some fixed income?

- If you choose variable income, which benchmark rate of return should you select (provided your annuity company provides a choice of rates)?

FIVE YEAR PLANS

Since there's no way to be sure how long you'll live and need income, some experts suggest making plans for five-year segments. That's long enough to see the effect of taking income from various sources during changing economic cycles. But it's short enough to catch potential problems and make adjustments in your spending style. This approach works well if you have the security of lifetime income for your basic needs.

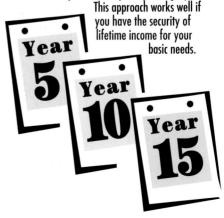

Know the Tax Penalties

THE TAX CONSEQUENCES

If you take a lump sum or periodic payments, you pay tax at your regular tax rate on the full amount of your earnings, which the tax law assumes are withdrawn first. That could reduce the amount you actually have to spend by up to 50% (in the highest federal and state brackets). If you annuitize a nonqualified annuity contract, part of each payment is a tax-free return of principal.

In addition, you'll want to remember that the assets in annuities and other retirement plans are put to better use providing you with income during your lifetime than serving as a way to benefit your heirs. One reason is that your beneficiaries also pay income tax on money they receive from the annuity contract to the extent that it exceeds the premiums.

Systematic Withdrawals

There's another way to get income from a deferred annuity.

If you own a deferred annuity that is still in the accumulation phase, chances are you'll have the option of setting up a systematic or periodic withdrawal program. Systematic withdrawal lets you receive income from the accumulated value of your contract on a regular schedule, making it an effective way to supplement your income either before or after retirement.

Systematic withdrawals are also flexible. Once you set them up, the money is paid regularly. But if you find you don't

need the cash, or if you want to change the amount, you can adjust the withdrawal arrangement simply by notifying the company. In addition, any amounts remaining in your contract continue to accumulate tax-deferred earnings.

But there are risks to systematic withdrawals. Chief among them is the possibility of depleting your assets more quickly than the rate at which they're growing. In a long retirement, you could run out of money.

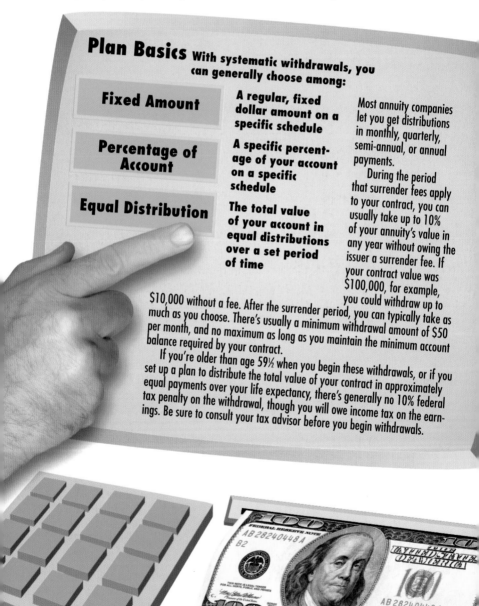

Plan Basics With systematic withdrawals, you can generally choose among:

Fixed Amount — A regular, fixed dollar amount on a specific schedule

Percentage of Account — A specific percentage of your account on a specific schedule

Equal Distribution — The total value of your account in equal distributions over a set period of time

Most annuity companies let you get distributions in monthly, quarterly, semi-annual, or annual payments.

During the period that surrender fees apply to your contract, you can usually take up to 10% of your annuity's value in any year without owing the issuer a surrender fee. If your contract value was $100,000, for example, you could withdraw up to $10,000 without a fee. After the surrender period, you can typically take as much as you choose. There's usually a minimum withdrawal amount of $50 per month, and no maximum as long as you maintain the minimum account balance required by your contract.

If you're older than age 59½ when you begin these withdrawals, or if you set up a plan to distribute the total value of your contract in approximately equal payments over your life expectancy, there's generally no 10% federal tax penalty on the withdrawal, though you will owe income tax on the earnings. Be sure to consult your tax advisor before you begin withdrawals.

MAKING A COMPARISON

Like choosing an income annuity, taking systematic withdrawals can be a convenient way to budget your money. You receive income in regular installments, just like receiving a paycheck. There are some important differences between systematic withdrawals and annuitization, though.

When you receive systematic withdrawals, you can generally stop the payments at any time, readjust the amount you receive, or select an entirely different withdrawal method. Annuitization, on the other hand, generally commits you to a specific income schedule, although new contracts tend to offer more flexibility, especially with specific term payout options. A **commutable contract**, for example, lets you stop or reduce your payout and take a lump sum.

Unlike a lifetime income annuity, however, a systematic withdrawal program doesn't promise payments for the rest of your life. Instead, you decide how much you want to receive on each payment date. Payments continue until you stop them or you run out of money. Then you have to look elsewhere for that portion of your retirement income.

There are tax implications, too. With systematic withdrawals, the tax code assumes you are receiving all your earnings first and get the principal back only after the earnings have been taken out. This means that payments in the early years will most likely be 100% taxable. That's known as the "last in, first out" rule.

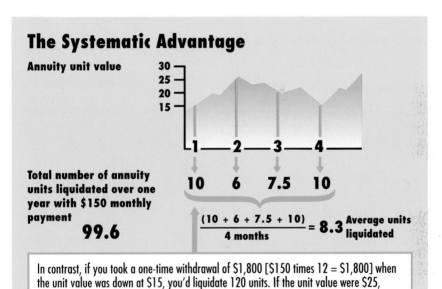

The Systematic Advantage

Annuity unit value

Total number of annuity units liquidated over one year with $150 monthly payment
99.6

$$\frac{(10 + 6 + 7.5 + 10)}{4 \text{ months}} = 8.3 \text{ Average units liquidated}$$

In contrast, if you took a one-time withdrawal of $1,800 [$150 times 12 = $1,800] when the unit value was down at $15, you'd liquidate 120 units. If the unit value were $25, you'd liquidate 72 units. However, there's no way to predict the value at any given time.

BETTER THAN RANDOM

When you withdraw money from your variable annuity account on a fixed schedule rather than taking it out randomly, you don't need to worry about whether or not it's the right time to liquidate.

The fact is, account values fluctuate continually, so there will always be times when accumulation unit values are higher and others when they're lower. If you're taking $150 each month, you'd liquidate six units if they're valued at $25 a unit, but ten units if they're valued at $15. Over time, the value will average out, so that while you are depleting the number of units you own, you're controlling the rate at which it happens.

USING MUTUAL FUND MONEY

You can also take systematic or periodic withdrawals from a mutual fund account to supplement your retirement income. Like withdrawals from annuity contracts, the payout terms are flexible, but you also run the risk of using up your assets while you're still alive.

If your mutual fund is a taxable investment, not part of a tax-deferred retirement plan, you can begin withdrawals anytime. As you withdraw, there may be realized capital gains on shares sold, and taxes you pay may be at the long-term capital gains rate rather than at your regular income tax rate, provided you have owned the fund for more than a year.

Other Ways to Get Income

You can get at the accumulated assets in your deferred variable annuity in various ways.

During the accumulation phase of a deferred variable annuity, you can take the accumulated assets as a **lump sum withdrawal**. Choosing that alternative means you're making a **full**, or **complete, surrender** of your contract rather than converting those assets to a source of continuing income.

You may have good reasons for taking a lump sum. For example, some grandparents use their annuity to pay for their grandchild's college education. Even after paying the taxes due, the tax-deferred earnings provided by the annuity can mean more money available for tuition and other bills.

Other reasons people give for taking a lump sum are to gain more day-to-day control over investing their money and to make sure that their assets don't end up reverting to the issuing company if they die shortly after payouts begin. This should not really be a concern, however, since most annuities provide income options that guarantee you will get most or all of your principal back. Most experts agree that while peace of mind is important, having to make smart investment decisions for a large amount of money can itself be a daunting task.

For retired people, the biggest drawback to lump sum withdrawals is the possibility of using up those assets during their lifetimes, being left with inadequate income.

USES FOR A LUMP SUM

College tuition for grandchild

Emergency medical expenses

PARTIAL SURRENDERS

During the accumulation phase, you can also take a portion of the accumulated value of your contract, or what is known as a **partial surrender**, if you need some of your assets, but want the rest to continue to grow. That preserves the opportunity to convert the balance to a stream of income later, yet allows you to meet an immediate need.

TIMING SURRENDERS

In addition to the tax penalty for taking money out of your contract before age 59½, you may owe surrender fees to the issuing company on withdrawals, although many contracts don't impose fees on the first 10% of the accumulated value. Those fees apply for a period of time following the purchase of the contract—typically seven to ten years. They're usually assessed on a declining scale, so that they disappear at the end of the period. In addition, the fees are often assessed on the premium only, not the gain. What's more, in many contracts, the surrender fees are based on the age of the premium, not the contract. In this case, the surrender period would be reset for each premium as it was paid. But some contracts impose no surrender fee.

Here's how the declining fee could apply:

Withdraw in year	1	2	3	4	5	6	7	8
Pay this percentage	7	6	5	4	3	2	1	0

Purchase price of entering a retirement center

Money to invest in a child's business or career

Money for nursing home expenses

TAXES ON LUMP SUMS

You'll owe income tax on all your earnings in the year you take a lump sum withdrawal. With nonqualified contracts, however, you owe no tax on your **cost basis**, or the premiums you paid when you bought the contract and any additional money you have added to it.

for example

If you put $40,000 into your annuity over a period of years, and its accumulated value is $95,000, you owe tax on the first $55,000 withdrawn.

Accumulated value	**$95,000**
Cost basis	**– $40,000**
Taxable amount	**= $55,000**

In computing the tax you owe, you add the taxable amount of the withdrawal to your other regular income. The risk is that the combined total may move you into a higher tax bracket for the year, increasing the percentage of tax that you pay.

In any case, owing tax means you end up with less money in your pocket—considerably less in a high bracket—than you might have expected based on the accumulated value of your annuity. And if you're younger than 59½ when you surrender your contract, you may have to pay an additional 10% federal tax penalty for early withdrawal. There are several exceptions to the penalty tax, including if you're using the money because you're disabled.

USING OTHER INCOME

In addition to your qualified retirement plans, such as a 401(k), and tax-deferred nonqualified plans, such as annuities, you may also have taxable investments, including stocks, bonds, mutual funds, and various cash accounts.

One approach is to set up a **systematic withdrawal** program for your taxable investments—your mutual funds, for example—in your early retirement years. This income, in combination with your Social Security benefits and employer pension if you have one, can help cover your expenses. If you've owned the investments at least one year, your gain will be taxed at the lower capital gains rate.

Meanwhile, your tax-deferred accounts can continue to compound until you're ready to add that income, or until you're required to begin making withdrawals from your qualified accounts at age 70½.

Planning Your Estate

One of your long-term goals may be enriching your heirs.

You can leave money to your children, grandchildren or other people who are important to you in a number of different ways. To make the transfers as easy and as financially sound as possible, it pays to know the advantages and disadvantages of naming beneficiaries, using wills and trusts, and owning property jointly. You should also review the types of assets you can transfer using each one.

Often the simplest thing to do is to make gifts of your assets while you're still alive. You can also transfer money to people by naming them as beneficiaries of your annuities, retirement plans, and insurance policies, by leaving them money in your will, or by making them the beneficiaries of one or more trusts. You can also make them joint owners of your assets, including real estate and other investments.

You also have to keep in mind that everything you own at your death (except what goes to your spouse or a charity) is considered part of the value of your estate. Your goal should be to minimize taxes on your estate by planning the transfers you want to make while you're alive.

However, the amount will be included in the total you're allowed to transfer tax free during your lifetime ($1 million) or at the time of your death (up to $1 million in 2002, increasing to $3.5 million by 2009). The tax-free amounts were set in the Economic Growth and Tax Relief Reconciliation Act of 2001. What happens, in effect, is that you can subtract the credit amount from the value of your transfers. Anything in excess of that is considered taxable.

NAMING BENEFICIARIES

You can name beneficiaries to any sources of income that are designed to be paid over your lifetime (such as annuities, IRAs or retirement plans) or at your death (life insurance).

When you die, those assets pass directly to the beneficiary you've named. They aren't included in your will and it is difficult for other heirs to contest your choice. What's more, there is no delay and no public record, as there is with a will.

Life insurance beneficiaries generally get a lump sum payment and may use the cash any way they wish, including buying an annuity to insure the income will last their lifetime. There is no income tax on the insurance amount they receive, though it is included in the value of your estate if you own the policy.

Beneficiaries of a tax-deferred plan owe tax on the earnings, but they may be able to choose the period of time over which they receive it. It generally pays to consult a tax specialist or other financial advisor for help in making the best choice. Remember, too, that the remaining value of the plan is included in your estate.

Give a $11,000 gift to anyone you want, TAX FREE

MAKING GIFTS

The good news is you can give anything you want to whomever you wish. In 2002, you can make a gift of up to $11,000 ($22,000 if you are married) to as many individuals as you wish without ever owing federal gift taxes on the amount. (The dollar value of the tax-free transfers you're allowed to make each year will increase if the inflation rate increases.)

If the value is higher than the annual limit, you can make the gift anyway.

CHARITABLE GIFTS

Tax-exempt gifts to charities aren't capped at $11,000, but the amount deductible annually for federal income tax purposes is limited to a percentage of your adjusted gross income. Be sure to consult your tax advisor before making a major gift.

**You can
pass your assets
to your beneficiaries through:**

- Your will
- An annuity
- IRAs and other
  retirement plans
- Life insurance

USING WILLS AND TRUSTS

You can transfer property using a will
or trust, or sometimes a trust that is
established in your will.

A **will** is a legal document that states
how your property is to be transferred
after you die. A will names:

- Your **heirs**, or the people who will
  inherit, and what you want them
  to receive
- Your **executor**, or the person who will
  handle the details of carrying out your
  wishes, called settling your estate
- A **guardian** who will take care of any
  minor children
- A **trustee** to administer any trusts
  the will establishes

A **trust** is a legal entity that you create
either while you are alive or in your will.
You transfer property to the trust and
name the people who will benefit from it
while it's in existence. Those people may
also assume ownership of the property
when the trust ends.

Trusts serve many purposes. They let
you manage your affairs and property
while you're still alive and instruct others
how you want them managed after your
death or during your lifetime if you are unable to do it yourself. They let you oversee
how assets are distributed to your heirs.
Finally, they can provide a way to reduce
potential estate taxes.

Using a will or a trust, your heirs
generally get their new possessions at a
step-up in basis, which means their
current market value. (This is not true for
annuities, including variable annuities.)
If your heirs sell the assets, they pay
tax on only the increases in value from
the day they inherited rather than the
increases from the date of original purchase. And that tax is paid at a **capital
gains rate**, which can be substantially
less than their regular income tax rate.

ESTATE TAXES

People try to avoid estate taxes because
they take a larger bite out of any assets
in excess of the tax-free amount that you
leave behind than even the highest income tax rate. In addition, some but not
all states impose inheritance taxes on the
value of your estate at rates that vary from
state to state.

If you're married and your spouse is
alive at your death, you can postpone the
tax by leaving everything to him or her.
But if assets in excess of the tax-free
amount remain when your spouse dies,
the taxes are then due.

THE BENEFITS OF LIFE INSURANCE

A sound life insurance strategy can help
eliminate the financial strain of having
to settle a taxable estate. Specifically,
getting the death benefit from your policy
means your
estate won't
have to sell
assets in order
to come up with
enough cash to
pay the tax. If
you estimate the
amount that will be
due, you can buy a
large enough insurance
policy to cover it.

FORM 706

**Postpone
estate taxes
by leaving
everything
to your
spouse.**

But a large life insur-
ance payout can have the
effect of increasing the size
of your estate. While your heirs don't pay
income tax on the settlement they receive
when you die, it could push your estate
value over the limit, so that estate taxes
will apply.

You can avoid this predicament,
though, by having someone else own the
policy on your life or by establishing a life
insurance trust to own it. This way, the
death benefit is paid outside your estate.
So not only is there money to pay any
estate tax that's due, but the value of the
estate won't be increased and therefore
subject to additional tax.

Charitable Annuities

You can combine financial planning with charitable giving.

In marshalling your sources of retirement income, you may want to consider a **charitable annuity** offered by an educational, cultural or charitable institution.

Charitable annuities resemble immediate annuities because they pay you income for life or for an extended term in return for a one-time payment. The key difference is that the money you use to buy the annuity is also a tax-deductible gift to the sponsoring institution.

To buy a charitable annuity, you can set up a **charitable living trust** or use a **charitable gift annuity**. You can work with your own financial advisor or with the institution offering the program. The college you attended and any museums, historical societies, religious organizations or other nonprofit organization you're affiliated with may have already sent you material describing their long-term giving program.

THE DONOR makes a tax-deductible gift and also buys an annuity.

SETTING INCOME

If you're considering a charitable annuity, you may debate which organization you want to benefit, but you don't have to comparison shop to get the most favorable income stream. That's because a group known as The Committee on Gift Annuities recommends uniform rates based on your age at the time you make your gift. Since the committee is sponsored by the organizations providing the annuities, the charities tend to adopt the recommendations.

HOW THE PLANS WORK

Charitable remainder trusts are designed specifically to provide both a tax deduction and regular income for you or someone you choose. You put assets in the trust and when the beneficiary dies (whether you or someone else), what remains in the trust becomes the property of the sponsoring institution.

A **charitable gift annuity** is an outright gift to the institution in return for a stream of income for you, or you and your spouse. The income you get depends on how old you are, the value of your gift, and whether the payout covers one or two lives.

The tax deduction you get for your gift is figured using the federal government's Estate and Gift Tax Valuation Tables. These tables take your life expectancy and the current interest rate into account in figuring your deduction. That's why the deductible amount may differ from the market value of your gift. That's one of the things your tax advisor can help you with.

WORKING TOGETHER

The idea behind charitable annuities is mutual benefit. The institutions that offer them depend on gifts to stay financially sound. The more assets these organizations can count on, the better the position they're in.

The people who choose charitable annuities get a steady source of income, an income tax deduction at the time they commit the money, and ultimately a way to reduce or avoid estate taxes. At the same time, they get the satisfaction of being benefactors of the institutions they admire.

THE CHARITY

uses the assets for its needs and pays you a lifetime income.

| Church | School | Museum |

If you don't have other heirs, or if you have enough money to benefit both your heirs and a nonprofit institution, these annuities can be a smart choice. One limiting factor, however, is that you generally need assets worth at least $50,000 to set up a trust. But the larger the gift, the more income it will produce.

HOW YOU BUY

You don't need cash to buy a charitable annuity. You can transfer stocks, bonds, real estate or even your retirement funds to the institution to establish the trust or annuity. The institution then takes the responsibility for paying you income from its assets, so that you don't have to worry about liquidating your own when you need money. And because the institution's asset pool is much larger, it can usually avoid having to sell when prices are down as someone might have to do in creating a regular income stream from a portfolio of equities.

TAXES ON ANNUITY INCOME

Part but not all of each annuity income payment you receive will be taxed at your ordinary tax rate. The portion that isn't taxed is considered return of principal, and is figured the same way it is with commercial annuities (see page 108). If you use appreciated property, such as stock, to buy the annuity, figuring the taxable portion is more complicated. In either case, the annuity sponsor should provide the information you need.

THE SMART ALTERNATIVE

While there are many ways to make substantial charitable gifts, annuities often make sense for this purpose.

For example, if you own stock that has increased in value over a number of years, you could sell it and give the cash to the institution. Or you could make a gift of the appreciated stock. The following examples help you compare what happens if you own 1,000 shares of stock that you bought for $25 a share and each share is now worth $125.

If you sell the stock, you would receive $125,000, and your capital gain would be $100,000 (before transaction fees). After paying $20,000 in tax at the long-term capital gains rate of 20%, you would have $105,000 left to make the gift.

If you gave the appreciated stock to the institution as part of arranging a charitable annuity, you could take a deduction for the gift and would owe no tax on the capital gain, thereby saving yourself $20,000. If you received even 5% of your gift as income for your lifetime —say $6,250 a year for 20 years—you would get back the entire $125,000 value of the gift. If you lived longer or the rate of return were higher, your total income would be higher.

In the meantime, the institution could either sell the stock (and reinvest the money) or let it continue to grow in value to meet future needs.

ANOTHER TRUST

You can also set up a **charitable lead trust**, but it won't provide a stream of income while you're alive. Instead, the charity gets the income produced by the assets in the trust for the time that the trust is in effect. When the trust ends, what's left in the trust goes to your heirs.

Mapping Out Your Approach

Flexibility and control are key to planning.

Nonqualified variable annuities are designed to play a part in your long-term retirement planning. You get tax-deferred growth on your investment earnings, and you can choose the way your money is allocated among the investment portfolios offered by the annuity contract you select.

What distinguishes variable annuities from other retirement planning tools are

- The opportunity to receive **lifelong** income
- The guaranteed death benefit that protects your premium payments and investment gains for your beneficiaries
- The flexibility to decide how much to contribute, how to allocate the money in your contract, and when to begin taking income
- The ability to change investment portfolios without owing income tax

What's more, you don't need to earn income to put money into a nonqualified variable annuity, as you do with an IRA or a qualified plan. So you can fund the annuity by contributing money you inherit or have gained from your investments.

A QUALIFIED DISTINCTION

Remember, if your variable annuity is a **qualified plan**, which means you're investing pretax dollars, the amount you can contribute and when you begin to withdraw are governed by special rules that apply to those plans. To be eligible for a qualified variable annuity, you typically have to work for an employer that offers one as part of your retirement savings package.

CHOOSING YOUR DIRECTION

Buying a nonqualified variable annuity involves making choices, but also gives you some control over the direction of your long-term retirement savings.

The more you understand about how an annuity works, the more informed choice you'll be able to make in selecting the best contract for you, as well as appropriate investment portfolios within the contract.

Of course, you can also buy a fixed annuity and not make any additional decisions, especially if you're making a one-time purchase. People who feel overwhelmed by financial matters or who are looking for a stable, guaranteed source of income do take that approach.

But if your preference is to stay attuned to what's happening with your investment portfolios, you have the opportunity to allocate your assets, monitor their performance, and change that allocation when it seems wise.

PROFESSIONAL MANAGEMENT

You allocate your variable annuity premiums among different investment portfolios managed by a specialist, or team of specialists, who make buy and sell decisions based on extensive research. That means you don't have to shoulder responsibility for that level of decision-making. You should, however, evaluate the past performance of these portfolio managers in making your investment decisions, as well as evaluating the performance of the portfolios themselves.

FLEXIBLE TIME LINES

Another advantage to nonqualified variable annuities is that there are fewer rules about how long you can continue to add money and when you must take it out. With most qualified retirement plans, you can put money in only as long as you have earned income and there are limits on what you can put in. In addition, you must begin taking income in the year following the one in which you turn 70½. With nonqualified annuities, on the other hand, you can build your account whether or not you're earning income, and you can often postpone withdrawals to age 85 or later.

UNLIMITED CONTRIBUTIONS

There are no federal or state limits on the amount of after-tax income you can add to your variable annuity each year. That's in direct contrast to what you can put into IRAs and qualified retirement plans. It means that variable annuities can help you build your nest egg faster.

	PAY IN	PAY OUT
Social Security	As long as you work	From 62, no advantage in waiting beyond 70
Pension	As long as you work	Typically when you retire
IRA	As long as you have earned income	Must begin by 70½
Annuity	As long as you want	Flexible by contract and state, often by 85

CONTRIBUTION LIMITS
Most retirement plans put strict annual limits on contributions.

IRA	$ 3,000 (for 2002–2004)
401(k)	$11,000 (for 2002)
	$12,000 (for 2003)
	$13,000 (for 2004)
Keogh	$40,000 (for 2002)
Nonqualified annuity	None

Investment Portfolios

Different annuities offer different portfolio choices.

If you've ever heard variable annuities described as mutual funds with insurance benefits, you may have some questions about what that means. The insurance you get is the opportunity to receive lifetime income and the assurance that your beneficiaries will receive a guaranteed death benefit if you die before taking income. In addition, some contracts offer enhanced benefits, such as locked-in gains, automatic asset reallocation, or a larger number of free transfers among your investment portfolios.

Just as an investment company offers a number of mutual funds, each with a specific investment objective, so a variable annuity offers a number of investment portfolios, each with a specific objective.

What you get with the annuity is the benefit of tax-deferred growth of earnings, something you achieve with a taxable investment only if you buy it through an IRA or qualified retirement plan. While you can put money directly into a mutual fund, however, you must buy the variable annuity contract before you can allocate money into the annuity's portfolios.

All variable annuity contracts offer an array of investment portfolios, including some that invest in stocks, some in bonds, and some in cash or cash equivalents. The actual number of portfolio choices, which can range from as few as six to three dozen or more, is less important, however, than the variety.

Some annuity owners might find a larger menu of choices intimidating. On the other hand, if you're interested in spreading your money across a range of investment options—an international portfolio as well as one that concentrates on small company stocks, for example—then the more choices you have, the closer you'll come to achieving the mix that you want.

TYPES OF PORTFOLIOS

Though variable annuity contracts offer different options, you'll typically have a choice among these major categories: equity (domestic and international), bond, money market, and balanced portfolios. Many contracts also have a fixed account.

EQUITY PORTFOLIOS

Growth is the overall objective of **equity portfolios**, which invest in stocks. Some equity portfolios focus on **aggressive growth**, which means making investments in companies that show promise of returns in the future but present greater financial risk than more established companies. In contrast, other portfolios concentrate on **growth and income** or **equity income**, which buy shares in stable, well-established companies that pay regular dividends but tend to grow at a more deliberate pace.

Sometimes a portfolio's name gives you an indication of how it is invested, for example "International Growth" or "Small Company Value". It's always smart, though, to read the description of both the portfolio's objective and investment approach in the prospectus.

Each contract typically offers at least one investment portfolio in each category, and frequently more than one. When there are more than one, each portfolio will have a somewhat different investment objective from the others as well as different strategies for achieving the portfolio's objectives. The roster of investments it holds will also be different. In this way, a portfolio can fit your allocation goals more precisely.

WHOSE FUNDS?

The investment portfolio choices in a variable annuity may be proprietary, which means they are provided by the insurance company issuing the annuity and are run by the company's investment managers.

FIXED ACCOUNTS

Fixed accounts pay a set rate of interest, and are very similar to fixed annuities. Although they are the least volatile, they offer less growth potential than other portfolio choices. Fixed portfolios tend to be most popular when annuity buyers are able to take advantage of high interest rates, or want to balance their more aggressive portfolios.

Or they may be investment portfolios managed by well-known mutual fund companies, investment advisory firms, brokerage firms, or banks and run by money managers working for those institutions.

Studies show that customers seem to be attracted to contracts offering brand names they recognize. To meet those expectations and to expand their offerings at the same time, companies are increasingly offering both proprietary and third party portfolio choices.

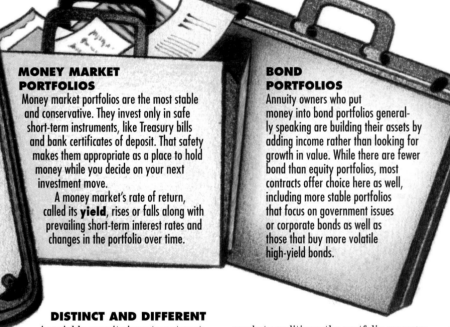

MONEY MARKET PORTFOLIOS

Money market portfolios are the most stable and conservative. They invest only in safe short-term instruments, like Treasury bills and bank certificates of deposit. That safety makes them appropriate as a place to hold money while you decide on your next investment move.

A money market's rate of return, called its **yield**, rises or falls along with prevailing short-term interest rates and changes in the portfolio over time.

BOND PORTFOLIOS

Annuity owners who put money into bond portfolios generally speaking are building their assets by adding income rather than looking for growth in value. While there are fewer bond than equity portfolios, most contracts offer choice here as well, including more stable portfolios that focus on government issues or corporate bonds as well as those that buy more volatile high-yield bonds.

DISTINCT AND DIFFERENT

A variable annuity investment portfolio may have a name that's similar to a particular mutual fund. But they're not the same funds, even if they share a manager. The money is never mingled. If both the portfolio and the fund buy the same investments, they buy separately. And they may, in fact, own different investments altogether.

Equally important, the two may produce different results. For example, an annuity portfolio and a similarly named mutual fund, both designed for long-term equity growth and run by the same manager, can post different returns. Since money may flow into an annuity on a more regular basis or be less apt to be withdrawn during changing

market conditions, the portfolio manager might make different investment choices than he or she would for a mutual fund, which needs more cash reserves available to redeem shares.

Balancing Your Annuity Account

It's smart to spread your assets among several investment portfolios.

If there's one investment guideline everyone agrees on, it's the importance of **diversification**. It means spreading your financial assets among a number of different investments, including stocks, bonds, real estate, annuities, mutual funds, and cash or cash equivalents.

If you concentrate on just one or two investments or investment categories, you risk taking a big hit if the performance of your particular choice falters. For example, if you have most of your mutual fund assets invested in small company growth, and that sector is in the doldrums, the value of your holdings could shrink.

What often makes diversification hard is that people have limited assets with which to diversify. By choosing a number of different investment portfolios offered through the annuity, you can get diversification even if the value of the contract is relatively modest.

LEVELS OF DIVERSIFICATION

With a variable annuity, it is possible to achieve substantial diversification since each contract offers a number of different investment portfolios, each of which is diversified as well. In putting some of your money into a growth portfolio that invests in large U.S. companies, for example, your return may reflect the performance of 100 or more companies.

If, in addition, you put money into a portfolio that invests in small companies, one that invests in international companies, and one that invests in technology, your assets will not only be spread across an even larger number of companies but you will be positioned to benefit from

those that tend to react positively to market conditions that may adversely affect stocks of large U.S. companies.

HOW YOU CHOOSE

There's no hard and fast rule about the number of portfolios it takes to be diversified. There is general agreement, though, about selecting a healthy overall portfolio:

- Since growth is important to achieving long-term goals, you should consider equity portfolios for a significant portion of your principal

- It makes more sense to choose two portfolios with different investment objectives than it does to choose two with the same objective

- Be careful about spreading your assets too thinly. The more substantial your holdings in any given portfolio, the more rapidly it can compound, earning you higher returns

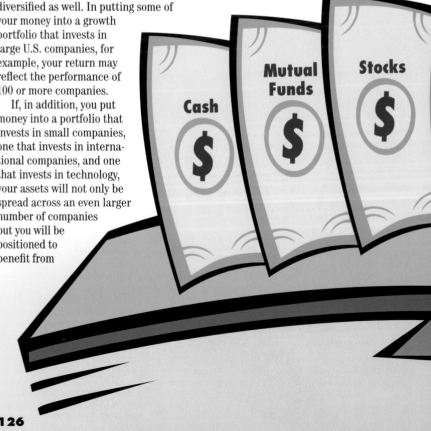

Cash

Mutual Funds

Stocks

OTHER WAYS TO DIVERSIFY

If choosing a number of different portfolios seems overwhelming, you might choose a **balanced** or an **asset allocation portfolio**, or use one or more **index portfolios**.

With a balanced portfolio, which invests in both equities and bonds, you enjoy the dual benefits of growth and income. While balanced portfolios may not achieve the same return as those that focus solely on equities, they're likely to retain more of their value in a down market.

Index portfolios make investments in order to mirror the performance of a market index such as the Standard & Poor's 500-stock index. Since index portfolios do not depend on the investment skills of a given portfolio manager, or on the performance of a particular segment of the market, many experts favor them, especially for new buyers. The risk, of course, is that in a falling stock market the decline in the portfolio's value would not be offset by holdings in bonds or cash equivalents as they could be in a balanced portfolio. Further, dropping values of a few large-company stocks in an equity index can have a major impact on index performance even if most stocks in the index are meeting expectations.

THINK ABOUT ALLOCATION

Another way to help guard against substantial loss of contract value is **asset allocation**. Basically it means assigning a percentage of your total assets to equities, a percentage to bonds, and a percentage to cash.

With variable annuities, for example, underlying investments react differently to changing economic conditions, and some perform better in certain circumstances than others. If you've spread your assets around carefully, there's a better chance that at least some of them will perform well even if others decline at any given time.

Historically, equities have provided much stronger returns than either bonds or cash, though they also tend to be the most volatile. To take advantage of this potentially higher return over the long haul, most experts suggest choosing equities for at least a portion of your total account value.

ONE ALLOCATION IDEA

A long-standing rule of thumb for allocating your investment assets has been to subtract your age from 100 and keep the balance in equity accounts. But more recent thinking is that such a balance may be appropriate for only the most conservative investors. This newer approach advocates keeping a minimum of 50% and perhaps more in equities.

Bonds

Annuities

Real Estate

Evaluating Annuity Performance

It's easy to get a handle on how a variable annuity is doing.

An important step in choosing an annuity contract and selecting your individual investment portfolios is evaluating **past performance**. While there's no guarantee of how well a portfolio will do in the future, past performance is one measure that's consistently used in assessing all kinds of investments. Often, the longer the history you have available, the better sense you can get of what might happen in the future because you can see how the portfolio has performed in different economic climates.

Another way to anticipate the future success of a portfolio is to review the prospectus for the types of investments it makes, the way it allocates its overall holdings, and the strategy of its portfolio manager. For example, an equity portfolio which buys large U.S. company stocks may generate slower but steadier earnings than a portfolio that buys stocks of small companies in emerging nations.

While your assessment is still a judgment call, it's more than a stab in the dark. The more consistent you are in your evaluation methods, the more patterns you'll begin to recognize. That's what financial professionals do in drawing their conclusions about the potential success of various investments.

THE KEY NUMBERS

When you assess portfolio performance, you look at the **total return** of the portfolio over specific periods of time. Total return is the annual profit after operating expenses for the portfolio, including any increase in price plus dividends or interest, stated as a percentage. For example, an investment may have an 8.5% total return.

When periods longer than a year are quoted, the return is **annualized**. That means it is converted to an annual basis. For example, if a portfolio's three year return is reported as 8.5%, that's the average of the returns for a three-year period. When you check performance reports, you're likely to find total returns reported for one, three, five, and ten year periods as well as the most recent month and the year to date (YTD).

MAKING COMPARISONS

The reason to check an investment portfolio's performance is that you can compare it to the performance of other portfolios in the same category. You can also compare performance to one or more **benchmarks**, or industry standards, such as the Lipper Annuity Indexes, provided by Lipper Inc.

Those equity and bond indexes are based on the performance of the largest investment portfolios within the group, usually 10 or 30, depending on the category. They show the percentage change in return for the group as a whole and the total value, in millions of dollars, of the portfolios included in the index.

With performance data, you can determine whether the portfolio you are considering measures up to what other, similar portfolios have done during the same period—or better yet, whether it has turned in a superior performance.

While it rarely makes sense to demand the star performance (since no portfolio is likely to be #1 year in and year out), what you're looking for are those that are consistently above average.

RESEARCHING A MANAGER

The investment strategy of the portfolio manager is described in the prospectus. The prospectus also explains the various measures that the manager might adopt to offset the risks of a high-yield bond portfolio, for example, or to protect an international equity portfolio's assets against currency fluctuation.

While investment styles or philosophies aren't in themselves a measure of performance, they can often help explain why a portfolio acts the way it does. For example, if an equity-fund manager concentrates on **value** stocks—those stocks whose prices are currently lower than they might be expected to be—the performance of the portfolio will follow a different pattern than that of a portfolio where the manager stresses rapid growth.

One of the reasons people are sometimes drawn to well-known, brand name portfolios is that their managers are often the subject of feature articles in the financial press, and may be quoted as experts on current economic trends. Putting your money into a portfolio managed by someone whose name you recognize can provide an extra measure of comfort though it's no guarantee of a strong return. It's also true that less well-known managers can be equally successful.

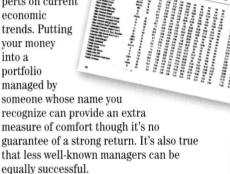

READ THE PAPER

A number of newspapers and periodicals report the performance of some variable annuity portfolios. Barron's, a weekly publication, lists the unit value, the four week total return, and one-year total return for hundreds of major insurers.

The Wall Street Journal reports on variable annuity performance every Monday. The coverage includes unit price, as well as one week and year to date total return and the expense ratio for the variable annuities it covers.

THE BIG PICTURE

For more detailed reports on investment portfolios, you can check the reports provided by professional information services. While subscriptions are available, you can generally find the materials in public libraries or online. Your financial planner or broker should also have access to these reports and be able to provide copies of the specific sections you want to read.

- **Variable Annuity Research and Data Service (VARDS), a service of Info-One.** There are four components

of The VARDS Report, which provides comprehensive monthly performance analysis on more than 14,000 investment portfolios, including risk-adjusted performance rankings. In addition, the report summarizes the content and pricing details of more than 480 variable annuity contracts, and provides research-based articles on subjects of current interest. There are also special reports on comparative contract expenses, sales and asset surveys, and other related subjects.

- **Morningstar.** Morningstar publishes the Variable Annuity Performance Report monthly. It posts performance figures for roughly 700 investment portfolios, with data going back as far as ten years. The report includes useful information, such as the advisor's name and phone number, fee structure information, net assets, and risk ratios.

- **Lipper Inc.** In addition to providing industry performance averages by portfolio category, such as those shown to the left, the firm publishes the Lipper Variable Insurance Products Performance Analysis Service. That

publication provides total return data for investment portfolios over different periods.

FEES AND CHARGES

It's important to remember that variable annuity performance is affected by fees and expenses such as the mortality and expense risk fee, administrative charges, and surrender charges if they apply. For more information on fees, see pages 132 to 135.

Keeping Up

You can—and should—continue to track your
portfolios' performances.

The performance information you used
to choose your investment portfolios to
begin with is equally valuable for keeping
track of how well those portfolios
continue to do.

WHAT'S TRACKED?

You can track the performance of
your investment portfolios because the
insurance company tracks the performance of each portfolio's **underlying
investments** and reports the overall
results weekly to the financial press.

Since performance figures change
constantly as the underlying investments
increase or decrease in value, the evaluation process is a dynamic one. It's also
relative, since current performance
figures are only meaningful in relation
to past performance of the same
portfolio, or the comparative
performance of one portfolio
with another.

WHAT IF YOU
DON'T TRACK?

Some people follow a hands-off policy
once they've chosen their investment
portfolios, often because they are uncomfortable with making financial decisions.
While their contracts may continue to
provide acceptable returns, experts caution that there is a potential downside to
this approach.

For example, if you had emphasized
bond portfolios when purchasing a contract in 1990 and transferred nothing to
equity portfolios over the next ten years,
you would have missed out on the
growth that accompanied the long
bull market during this period.

CALL THE COMPANIES

Most annuity companies have toll-free
numbers you can call to get performance
figures on individual portfolios within your
variable annuity. Some lines are automat-
ed, so you can check in 24 hours a day,
seven days a week. In addition, many
companies update performance figures
on their websites on a regular basis.

That doesn't mean you should
hover over the phone or stay glued
to the screen. Like all investments,
an annuity portfolio, especially an
equity portfolio, may be volatile in the
short term, moving higher or lower to

reflect the performance of its underlying
investments.

Since an annuity is a long-term commitment, what really matters is a pattern
of performance over time. In fact, the
longer the time frame that's covered, the
better you can tell how the portfolio may
do in up and down markets. Daily changes
are far less relevant.

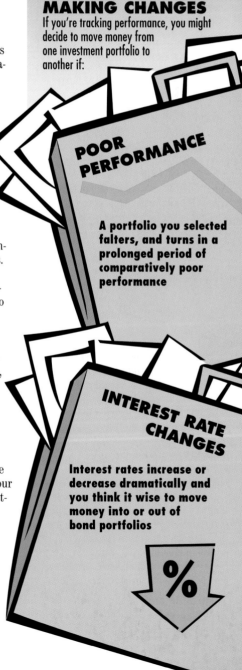

MAKING CHANGES

If you're tracking performance, you might
decide to move money from
one investment portfolio to
another if:

POOR PERFORMANCE

A portfolio you selected
falters, and turns in a
prolonged period of
comparatively poor
performance

INTEREST RATE CHANGES

Interest rates increase or
decrease dramatically and
you think it wise to move
money into or out of
bond portfolios

One approach to financial planning is to set aside one day a year to reassess where you stand. Some people do it on January 1—to start the new year on the right foot.

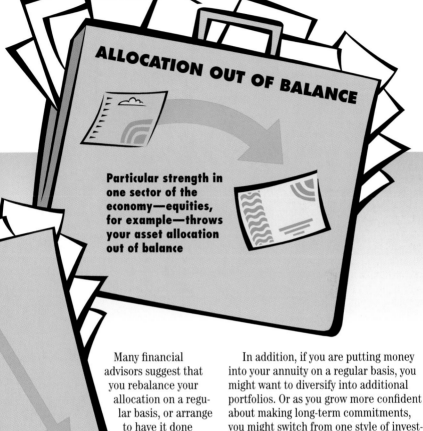

ALLOCATION OUT OF BALANCE

Particular strength in one sector of the economy—equities, for example—throws your asset allocation out of balance

Many financial advisors suggest that you rebalance your allocation on a regular basis, or arrange to have it done automatically by the issuer. They suggest you rebalance both during the accumulation phase of a deferred variable annuity and after you begin to take variable income.

NO SWEAT, NO TEARS

It's relatively easy to transfer assets from one investment portfolio to another within a contract. There are no income tax consequences when you make such a change, and most contracts permit a number of free transfers each year. That's one of the features that people find attractive about a variable annuity.

In addition, if you are putting money into your annuity on a regular basis, you might want to diversify into additional portfolios. Or as you grow more confident about making long-term commitments, you might switch from one style of investing to another. For example, you might begin by putting a large amount of money into a money market portfolio because it seems safe. But if you track the returns on that portfolio and on a portfolio investing in U.S. stocks, you might decide you'd be better off moving some of your assets so that you could benefit from the potentially stronger performance of the equities.

NO VARIABLE PROJECTIONS

As you evaluate past performance of variable annuity portfolios, what you won't find are projections of future performance. That's because there is no way to provide those numbers.

Such projections are customary, though, for a fixed annuity contract and for the fixed account within your variable contract. Since the issuing company knows for certain what the current interest rate is, what the guaranteed floor is, and what a best-case scenario is, the levels of growth that those various numbers will produce can be computed.

What You Pay

There are some costs involved with owning variable annuities.

Fees are another factor to consider in selecting a variable annuity contract. They can differ depending on the services and benefits the contract provides.

Some fees are associated with administering the variable annuity contract, which is also referred to as a **separate account**. Other fees are used to provide insurance benefits, and still others to offset the costs of managing the investment portfolios. When the portfolios are proprietary, the fund management fees are paid to the insurance company that issues the contract. When the portfolios are managed by other financial institutions, the fees are paid to them.

What you actually end up paying in fees depends on the contract you select and the way you allocate your assets within the contract. Most experts agree that cost shouldn't be the only reason for selecting a contract or an individual investment portfolio. It's also important to look at the benefits and services the annuity contract provides, as well as the performance of their investments.

ANNUAL AND ASSET-BASED FEES

Fees are calculated on either an annual or an asset basis, and both types apply to variable annuity contracts.

Annual fees are fixed expenses that are deducted from your contract account value and average about $30 a year.

Asset-based fees are a percentage of the total value of your annuity (other than money allocated to the fixed account), deducted on a daily basis. All owners of the same contract pay the same percentage of their assets in these fees, but different dollar amounts.

Many contracts waive the annual fees when your account reaches a certain value, generally between $25,000 and $50,000. But the larger your account grows, the more total dollars you'll pay in asset-based fees.

MORTALITY AND EXPENSE FEE

The asset-based mortality and expense risk (M&E) fee that is charged on all variable annuity contracts pays for four things:

1. The guaranteed death benefit
2. The option of a lifetime payout
3. The assurance of fixed insurance costs, including the M&E fee itself, which are frozen for the life of the contract
4. The guarantee of minimum annuity purchase rates when you annuitize

Handwritten note on deposit slip:

WHAT YOU PAY:
Administration fee
Insurance benefit fees
Surrender fees
Fund management fees

Customer's Order No.

KEEP THIS SLIP FOR REFERENCE

Handwritten note on second deposit slip:

Fund management fee due to outside institution

Customer's Order No.

KEEP THIS SLIP FOR REFERENCE

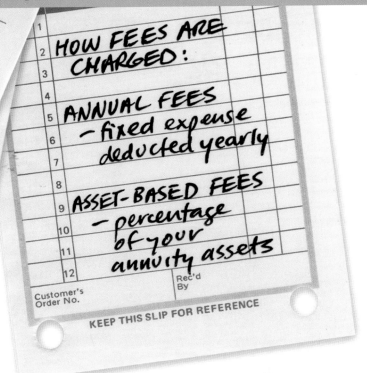

HOW FEES ARE CHARGED:

ANNUAL FEES
- fixed expense deducted yearly

ASSET-BASED FEES
- percentage of your annuity assets

KEEP THIS SLIP FOR REFERENCE

The cost of these **insurance features** typically ranges up to 1.5% of the total value of your variable annuity each year, with the 2000/2001 average at 1.158% according to VARDS. In most cases, the fee is subtracted proportionally from each of the variable portfolios into which you've put money.

When comparing a number of contracts, you'll find that sometimes the M&E fee is higher than average, while administrative and maintenance fees are lower, or vice versa. Experts suggest that what you look at is the entire fee package, rather than any single component, in evaluating a contract.

MORE BENEFITS/MORE COST

A number of variable annuity contracts offer features often described as **enhanced benefits**. One such benefit is a more generous death benefit guarantee, which locks in any portfolio gains for payment to your beneficiary should you die during the accumulation phase. Another new benefit is additional protection for your income payments during retirement. These **guaranteed minimum income benefits** ensure a minimum lifetime income stream when you **annuitize**, or convert the savings in your annuity into income payments. Still other new features, such as long-term care protection, are also being offered.

In general, you pay for these enhancements in additional fees. The fees generally reflect the nature and extent of the risks and expenses the company is assuming in providing these extra services.

STEPPED UP DEATH BENEFITS

Initially, the death benefit guarantee provided that your beneficiary would receive the greater of your contract value or the amount of your premium (minus any withdrawals) if you died during the accumulation phase of your variable annuity. Today, some insurers have added new features to make their annuities more competitive and attractive. This means the cost of the death benefit feature may be higher. You have to decide whether the additional protection is worth the additional fee.

There are other new features as well. The insurer might guarantee payment of the premium amount, plus a fixed annual rate of interest. For example, if you put $100,000 into an annuity, your beneficiary would be entitled to at least that amount, plus perhaps 4% interest compounded annually or whatever the rate specified in the contract might be.

Some insurers offer a death benefit feature that allows you to lock in your investment gains every year or every few years. For example, if your variable annuity contract increased from $100,000 to $142,500 by its fifth anniversary date, many contracts lock in that $142,500 as the new minimum death benefit guarantee. Even if your annuity dropped in value in the following year, your beneficiary would still be entitled to the $142,500.

More about Fees

There's a lot to be said for the concept of getting what you pay for.

Some fees pay directly for the insurance benefits that a variable annuity contract provides. Other fees pay for operating the individual investment portfolios.

MANAGEMENT FEES

Asset-based management fees are used to pay the investment portfolio manager as well as other expenses associated with operating a portfolio. These fees are described in the prospectus, and are sometimes broken down into an investment advisory fee and an operating expense fee. Other times, they're aggregated under the management fees heading. These fees don't appear as a separate figure on your regular statements but are reflected in your portfolio values.

While operating fees average about 0.77% annually, the actual charge can vary quite dramatically, based on the size of the fund or the way the portfolio invests. For example, fees on index portfolios tend to be significantly lower than the norm because the management costs are lower. On the other hand, fees on international equity portfolios or those requiring extensive research and oversight tend to be higher. These fee structures tend to be

fairly consistent from contract to contract. They're also comparable to, but generally lower than, the management fees you pay as part of a mutual fund investment.

If you put some of your money into a fixed account within your variable annuity contract, the expenses are paid by the account's **interest margin**. This margin is the difference between the percentage being earned on investments made by the company and the percentage being paid to you as earnings.

EXPENSE RATIOS

Another way to analyze the cost of an annuity contract is to look at its **expense ratio**. Expense ratios are the total expenses, expressed as a percentage, that you pay for the insurance and management costs of the total assets in your annuity. The expense ratio can be found in the prospectus and is published regularly in performance reports that appear in the financial press.

The average expense ratio, including management and contract fees, is 2.14%. You can check the expense ratio figures on your own, and you can also ask for that information from the insurance company or your financial advisor.

Even for portfolios offered by a single annuity contract, you'll notice that the difference in expense ratios can be signifi-

Fund Name	Unit Price	%Total Ret i-wk	YTD	Tot Exp	Am
VARIABLE INSURANCE CO					An
BIG EDGE PLUS (THE)					An
Asia					Ar
Balanced	0.500	0.03	−24.95	2.50	Ar
Bond	1.880	1.12	8.64	1.96	Ar
Enhanced Index	3.900	−0.90	−3.17	1.90	An
Growth	1.210	1.00	14.99	1.25	Ce
International	12.240	1.67	13.74	1.99	Dr
Real Estate	2.200	1.69	25.05	2.26	F
Strategic	1.560	0.63	−15.74	2.25	F
Strategic Asst All	1.433	1.63	13.48	2.25	F
Templ Asst All 2	4.797	1.18	8.48	1.96	
Templ Dev Mkt 2	1.113	1.17	3.44	2.28	
Templ Intl 2	0.447	0.44	−33.00	3.02	
Templ Stock 2	1.160	1.46	7.82	2.38	
Wanger Intl Sm Cap	1.072	0.55	0.97	2.39	
Wanger Small Cap	1.877	−0.87	10.83	2.85	
LIFE & HEALTH INS CO					
VANGUARD VA PLAN	2.256	−0.21	5.45	2.31	
Balanced	25.191	0.16	5.23	0.7	

cant. Those variations are the result of differing management expenses.

Though you probably won't want to choose your investment portfolios on

SURRENDER FEES

Under many variable annuity contracts, there's a charge, or **surrender fee**, if you withdraw part or all of your contract value during the early years of the contract. These surrender fees are usually calculated as a percentage of the amount of the withdrawal. However, many annuities let you withdraw a certain percentage of your account value each year without a surrender fee.

For example, if you withdraw any money from your variable annuity account in the first year, your surrender fee might be 7%. This percentage generally declines each year until the fee disappears, typically seven years after the purchase. With some contracts, the surrender fee period begins with the purchase of the contract. With others, a new surrender fee period begins with each new purchase payment.

Surrender fees serve several purposes. First, they make people think twice before taking their money out, and thereby interrupting the growth of their long-term retirement account.

The fee also benefits the insurance company that issues the annuity contract. The company has significant expenses for sales and marketing of the annuity, insurance underwriting, and other costs. So it counts on receiving asset-based fees or interest margin over a period of years. The surrender fees cover the loss of income that results when an annuity is ended earlier than projected.

HERE AND THERE

A few states impose a premium tax on amounts you use to purchase an annuity contract, whether you make a single payment or pay periodically. Those charges may be up to 4% of the premium, but more typically run around 2%. They're independent of any fees the insurer or management company charges.

In some cases, however, you may find that the way retirement income is taxed in those states that impose a premium can ultimately offset the added upfront cost of buying the annuity.

expense ratio alone, it should be one of the factors you consider, particularly when choosing among those with comparable performance records.

IS THERE AN AX TO GRIND?

Variable annuities are sometimes criticized as more costly to own than other investments. The critics point out that mutual funds, which also involve asset-based fees, have expense ratios averaging 1.37%, in comparison to the 2.14% that's typical of variable annuities, based on data provided by Morningstar's Principia Service as of December 2000. Those costs, for example, mean that an equity portfolio within an annuity contract must turn in a consistently stronger performance in order to provide the same level of return.

What these observations ignore are the very things that help make variable annuities appealing, including:

- The fact that the returns on annuity portfolios are tax-deferred
- The option of receiving guaranteed retirement income for life
- Insurance features, such as the death benefit
- A guarantee that insurance expenses will not increase above certain limits
- Advice available from financial advisors who sell the annuities

An Annuity Who's Who

It helps to recognize the cast of characters.

Every nonqualified variable annuity has a cast of players, including the owner, the insurance company, an annuitant, and a beneficiary. Their relationships to each other are spelled out in the contract.

The players and their roles tend to be consistent from contract to contract, so once you understand the part each one plays you can use that information to make your own variable annuity decisions.

THE OLDER YOU GET

The curious thing about life expectancy is that the older you get, the longer you can expect to live. If you're 65, you'll typically live until you're 85, but if you are 75, your life expectancy is another 12½ years, or 87½. If you live until 87½, you can expect—statistically—to live until you're 93.

If you live until 93 or even 103, a variable annuity that guarantees lifetime income will pay that long, no matter what your life expectancy was at the time your payments began.

The Owner

The owner buys the annuity by paying a premium, or sum of money to the issuer

OWNING A CONTRACT

If you buy a nonqualified variable annuity, you select the contract and name the annuitant and the beneficiary. You also allocate the premium among the investment portfolios offered through the contract. Finally, you decide how and when the annuitant will receive income.

If you're buying the contract as part of your long-term retirement savings strategy, typically you'll be the annuitant as well as the owner. You might plan to receive income for your life, or designate your spouse as a joint annuitant, so that the contract could provide income to last through both your lifetimes.

There are circumstances, though, when you might buy a contract to provide income for someone else—a parent, for example, or a disabled child—for whom you have financial responsibility. In those cases, you would be the owner but not the annuitant.

The Company

The insurance company issues the contract and agrees, in return for the premium, to accept certain financial and administrative responsibilities

THE COMPANY

An insurance company, either by itself or as part of an agreement with another financial institution (such as a mutual fund company), offers variable annuity contracts and assumes a number of responsibilities on behalf of the owners. Those jobs include administrative tasks such as providing regular account information, and financial duties such as assuring that premiums are invested according to an owner's wishes.

The responsibility that's unique to an insurance company is standing behind the guarantees in an annuity contract, such as the death benefit and the option of an income you can't outlive.

OTHER OWNERS

Though a person is typically an annuity owner, there are others—a trust, partnership, corporation, or employer—who can own a contract naming a specific person as annuitant. If it is an immediate or qualified annuity, or if a deferred contract ends up in your estate, there's no problem since the owner is considered to be acting as an agent for the annuitant.

However, if a trust, partnership, or corporation owns a nonqualified annuity purchased since 1986, the earnings are taxable each year, effectively wiping out the tax advantages of owning a contract.

MAKING A GIFT

While you typically buy an annuity to provide retirement income for yourself and your spouse, you can put the tax-deferred growth that annuities provide to work for younger people as well. For example, you might buy each of your grandchildren a single premium annuity on their 10th birthday, explaining that it's a start on building their own retirement security—even if that's 55 or more years away.

As long as the premium is less than the annual ceiling on tax-exempt gifts, there are no tax consequences for you, and none for the recipient until he or she begins to take income.

The Annuitant

The annuitant is typically the person designated to receive income from the contract and whose life expectancy is used as the basis for figuring lifetime payments

BEING AN ANNUITANT

An annuitant is usually the person named in the contract to receive income from the annuity. While the annuitant doesn't make contract decisions as the owner does, who the annuitant is has a major impact on the terms of the contract. Unlike the owner, the issuer, or the beneficiary, the annuitant must be an actual (living) person, typically age 75 or younger at the time the annuity is purchased.

The annuitant is important to the variable annuity contract because his or her life expectancy when the income payments begin is key to setting the amount of the annuity payments. The annuitant's life expectancy also affects the percentage of each payment that will be taxable.

The annuitant's life expectancy for those tax purposes is determined using tables issued by the Internal Revenue Service (IRS). For example, if the annuitant's age is 65, his or her life expectancy is 20 years, until age 85.

The Beneficiary

The beneficiary receives the death benefit if the annuitant, or the owner, depending on the contract, dies before the income period begins

BENEFICIARY

The beneficiary receives a death benefit from the annuity contract if the annuitant or owner dies before the income payments begin. The contract also pays the beneficiary when income payments are guaranteed for a certain period and the annuitant dies before that amount of time has passed.

The beneficiary can be a person or persons (including the owner if he or she is not the annuitant), a charity, or a trust. The contract owner names the beneficiary and usually has the right to change that designation at any time.

Most annuity contracts allow the owner to list multiple beneficiaries, so that the death benefit or income can be divided among them when the annuitant dies. When there are multiple beneficiaries, the owner must assign a percentage value of the annuity to each beneficiary. That's because it's impossible to predict what the dollar value of the annuity assets will be over time. By using a percentage, each beneficiary gets a proportionate share. For example, a mother might name her son as beneficiary of 50% and her daughter as beneficiary of the remaining 50%. That way, the assets could be shared evenly, in keeping with the mother's wishes.

Annuity Providers

There's enormous choice among variable annuities.

Insurance companies create variable annuity products either on their own or in an agreement with other financial services companies, and offer them for sale through a variety of outlets known as **distribution channels**. These channels include insurance agents, brokerage firms, investment advisors registered with the National Association of Securities Dealers (NASD), banks and credit unions, and mutual fund companies.

Selling variable annuities is an active business. By mid-2001, more than 100 companies offered these products, giving buyers a choice of more than 480 separate contracts that together offer more than 14,000 investment portfolios.

HANDLING BUSINESS

The issuing company has an ongoing relationship with people like you who buy one of its products. The company provides the prospectus, the actual contract, and periodic statements that detail the transactions in your contract, including premium payments, transfers, surrenders, and contract-based fees. Or, if you have a number of different accounts with a financial services institution such as a bank, a brokerage firm, or a mutual fund company, you may receive a consolidated statement for all your accounts, including the annuity.

The insurance company also explains the various ways you can take income from your annuity and the tax consequences of these choices. And when you do start taking the income, the company handles all of those details as well, including figuring the number of units you own and their changing value. The company also computes the amount of each income payment and oversees delivery of that amount. The income services, which simplify what can otherwise be a major hassle, are often cited as a major appeal of owning an annuity.

Insurance companies also maintain customer service departments to handle questions about the annuities they offer as well as their other insurance products. If you're making periodic payments, the company sends reminders when additional premiums are due.

INVENTION AND REINVENTION

The basic elements of any annuity contract are similar: tax-deferred earnings, a range of investment portfolios, a guaranteed death benefit, and the opportunity to have the accumulated assets paid out as lifetime income.

What distinguishes one contract from the other are special features that an issuing company offers to make the product more attractive to purchasers. Examples include enhanced death benefits, a broader range of investment portfolios, and built-in management aids such as automatic allocation and re-allocation of portfolio assets and internal dollar cost averaging, plus flexible purchase arrangements.

DEFINING TERMS

Simply explained, a **security** is evidence of ownership or the rights to ownership, such as a stock or bond. **Insurance** is a system in which you pay premiums so that you or your beneficiary can collect payment in a clearly defined situation.

MULTIMANAGER PRODUCTS

A growing trend in variable annuities is multimanager contracts, which offer portfolios run by a number of different managers in addition to those administered by the issuing company.

Sometimes, when an insurance company and a distributor, such as a bank or a brokerage firm, work closely together, they offer variable contracts that include investment portfolios bearing just the issuing company's or the bank's name. In other cases, a single contract might offer individually managed portfolios provided by outside sources, including mutual fund companies.

The more portfolio choice there is within a contract, the more opportunity individual buyers have to allocate their assets in ways that suit their goals and their tolerance for risk.

THE ROLE OF REGULATION

Variable annuities are considered securities, like stocks and bonds, as well as insurance products. Variable annuities that are registered with the U.S. Securities and Exchange Commission (SEC) are sold with the benefit of a prospectus that provides full disclosure of the objectives, management, and fees. In addition, they can be sold only by registered representatives of brokerage

firms that are members of the National Association of Securities Dealers (NASD). As insurance, contracts sold in a particular state are regulated by the laws of that state, and fall under the jurisdiction of the state insurance departments.

Rating Annuity Providers

Rating services give you a report card on your annuity provider.

One of the primary considerations in choosing an annuity is establishing whether the provider is going to be able to meet its long-term commitments to you.

Often the keys to this assessment are the company's past performance and its current financial situation. Fortunately you don't have to hunt down that information on your own. Several professional rating services, including A.M. Best Company, Moody's Investors Service, Standard & Poor's, Fitch, Inc., and Weiss Research, evaluate providers and publish their findings on a regular basis. While not all insurance companies are rated, enough are to give you ample data on a wide range of choices.

WHY RATINGS MATTER

Ratings are especially important when you're choosing a fixed annuity because your premiums go into the company's general account. If the company has financial problems, you're not insulated from the company's potential losses. So the stronger the company is, the more comfortable you can feel about purchasing a fixed annuity from it.

The same situation applies to the fixed account you might have in a variable annuity. That portion of your retirement savings is handled the same way as a fixed annuity contract is. So ratings matter in this case as well.

On the other hand, when you put money into any of the other investment portfolios of a variable annuity, your principal goes into a separate account that is insulated from claims against the company (though not against the ups and downs of the underlying markets). The security of your assets in the separate account is pegged to the risk and performance of the underlying investments in the investment portfolios and not the insurer's financial strength.

So it may seem that ratings are less important. But since you may be relying on the insurance company to pay you lifetime income, taking a company's rating into account when choosing a variable annuity contract makes sense as well.

HOW THEY RATE

While each rating service has its own proprietary system for evaluating annuity providers, they generally focus on the following rating factors:

- Claims-paying ability, or the likelihood of the insurer's making good on its insurance obligations
- Company strength, which is a measure of the company's financial reserves stored up to pay out claims
- Financial history, which looks at whether the company has had problems with insolvency, or an inability to pay its own debts when they are due
- Soundness of the company's general account investments

HANDING OUT GRADES

Each service assigns a rating to each insurance company it evaluates, typically as a letter grade. The oldest rating service, A.M. Best, measures a company's relative financial strength and its ability to meet its obligations with ratings that range from the high of A++ to the low of C–. Companies with an A++ rating are considered superior and those with an C– are considered extremely weak.

Rating	A.M. BEST
Superior	A++, A+
Excellent	A, A–
Good	B++, B
Adequate	B, B–
Below average	C++, C+
Weak	C, C–
Non-viable	D, E, F

WHERE TO FIND RATINGS

You can get an overview of many of the company ratings by scanning the websites of the various services. If you want to read the more detailed analysis, you can find copies of current rating reports in many local libraries or ask your financial planner or broker to provide the ones you want. Insurance companies will also provide a copy of a report if you request one.

In addition, you can contact the different services by telephone to request the information you want, though there may be a charge in some cases.

- A.M. Best. 908-439-2200. $19.95 for Best's Company Reports. $4.95 for a company rating. (www.ambest.com)
- Standard & Poor's. 212-438-2400. No charge, three insurer ratings per call. (www.standardpoor.com)
- Fitch. 800-853-4824, ext. 199. No charge for rating. Company report costs $25. (www.fitchratings.com)
- Moody's. 212-553-0377. No charge, four ratings reports per call. (www.moodys.com)
- Weiss Research. 800-289-9222. $15 per company over the phone. One-page written ratings available for $25 per company. A fuller 25-page company report costs $45. (www.weissratings.com)

THE RAW MATERIAL

The information the rating services use to evaluate annuity providers comes in part from the public record and in part from the companies themselves. Some of it is **quantitative**, based on mathematical computations that the rating services have devised and some is **qualitative**, based on an assessment of management style, investment strategy, and other factors.

Other services, like Standard & Poor's and Fitch, which assess claims-paying ability, use a rating system similar to those used for rating bonds, which is also based on letter codes. For these two providers, a superior rating is AAA, and the lowest acceptable is B–. Moody's, which measures financial strength and the company's ability to pay, uses a different style, with the highest rating being Aaa and the lowest B3.

In general, a company ranked excellent by one rating service is likely to receive a similar, though not necessarily identical, ranking from another. That's because the rating services use somewhat different criteria in making their assessments. So it's generally a good idea to look at the ratings from at least two of the services when you are comparing companies.

STANDARD & POOR'S	MOODY'S	FITCH	WEISS RESEARCH
AAA	Aaa	AAA	
AA+, AA, AA–	Aa1, Aa2, Aa3	AA+, AA, AA–	A
A+, A, A–	A1, A2, A3	A+, A, A–	B
BBB+, BBB, BBB–	Baa1, Baa2, Baa3	BBB+, BBB, BBB–	C
BB+, BB, BB–	Ba1, Ba2, Ba3	BB+, BB, BB–	D
B+, B, B–	B1, B2, B3	B+, B, B–	E
CCC, CC, R	Caa, Ca, C	CCC, CC, C, DDD, DD, D	F

Buying and Selling Annuities

Annuity buyers and annuity sellers need each other.

Whether you're in the market for an immediate or deferred variable annuity as part of your individual retirement planning, you can take a similar approach in identifying the salesperson you'll work with, selecting the specific annuity you'll buy, and deciding on the investment portfolios into which you want to put your money.

HOW MUCH CHOICE?

Your choice of annuity contracts will depend on where you buy. For example, a direct seller, such as a mutual fund company, may offer only its own products. A brokerage firm or bank, on the other hand, usually has business arrangements with a number of different insurance companies to offer their products. Typically, you'll have access to a wide range of features available in different contracts.

GETTING STARTED

If you're interested in buying an annuity, you may want to contact your financial advisor or a financial institution you're already doing business with, such as an insurance company, a bank, brokerage house, or mutual fund company. Or you may learn about annuities and the role they can play in your retirement planning through an individual meeting with an annuity salesperson, a financial planning seminar or a presentation sponsored by a local library or other organization.

Remember, nothing has to be done on the spot, so you don't have to feel pressured to act immediately. The written information you're provided—for example, the prospectus—should answer the questions you have, especially those concerning the best investment portfolios for you. In addition, the salesperson you're working with should be ready—and willing—to answer your questions. So don't hesitate to ask.

WHERE THE MONEY'S GOING

In choosing among the various portfolios available in variable annuity contracts, buyers overall allocate slightly more than 64% of their assets to equity portfolios and an additional 7.7% to balanced or asset allocation portfolios, which themselves typically own at least 50% equities. While equity portfolios can be more volatile than fixed accounts, they are able to provide inflation protection and long-term growth potential—primary goals of retirement savings plans.

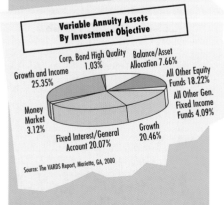

Variable Annuity Assets By Investment Objective

Corp. Bond High Quality 1.03%
Balance/Asset Allocation 7.66%
Growth and Income 25.35%
All Other Equity Funds 18.22%
All Other Gen. Fixed Income Funds 4.09%
Money Market 3.12%
Fixed Interest/General Account 20.07%
Growth 20.46%

Source: The VARDS Report, Marietta, GA, 2000

BUYING A QUALIFIED ANNUITY

If your employer offers a variable annuity as part of a qualified retirement savings plan, you can have the premium deducted from your salary in regular amounts during the year—or until you've reached the maximum possible contribution. If your employer matches a percentage of your contribution, be sure you're taking full advantage of this policy. Your employer should tell you what level of contribution to make and over what period of time, to maximize the benefit.

For example, if the match covers a certain percentage of your contribution—say up to 6% of your salary—it makes sense to put in at least 6%. And if there's a limit on the dollar amount that your employer will match in any single pay period, you can spread out your contribution over the year so that you qualify for the maximum matching amount.

QUALIFIED SELLERS

Variable annuities are sold by registered representatives of brokerage firms that are members of the National Association of Securities Dealers (NASD). In addition, the registered representatives must meet insurance license requirements for each state in which they work, and are often registered with the Securities and Exchange Commission (SEC) as registered investment advisors, or RIAs. There are also continuing education requirements that representatives need to maintain their licenses.

BROKER/DEALERS

Registered representatives who sell annuities are either affiliated directly with an insurance company (these representatives are known as captive agents) or with a **broker/dealer**. That term describes a securities firm or other financial institution that acts as an intermediary between insurance companies that provide annuities and the individuals who buy them. Typically, a broker/dealer has alliances with a number of companies, so its registered representatives can sell you any of the products issued by any of these **companies**.

Broker/dealers are responsible for supervising the work of their representatives, providing sales literature and materials, and deciding which products to market.

WHERE YOU BUY

If you're in the market for a nonqualified annuity, you can buy through:

- **A bank**
- **A national or regional brokerage firm**
- **A financial planner affiliated with an independent NASD broker/dealer**
- **An agent working with a specific insurance company**
- **Direct provider or marketer, typically a mutual fund**

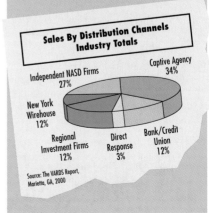

Sales By Distribution Channels Industry Totals

Independent NASD Firms
27%

Captive Agency
34%

New York Wirehouse
12%

Regional Investment Firms
12%

Direct Response
3%

Bank/Credit Union
12%

Source: The VARDS Report, Marietta, GA, 2000

accumulation units: The shares of ownership you have in a variable annuity investment portfolio during the period you are saving for retirement. As you pay additional premiums, you buy additional units.

annuitant: The person who receives income from an annuity. The annuitant's life expectancy is used to figure the initial income amount the annuity pays.

annuitize: To convert the accumulated value of an annuity into a stream of income, either for one or more lifetimes or a specific period of time.

annuity contract: A legal agreement between you and an insurance company, sometimes called an annuity company.

annuity units: The number of units you own in a variable annuity investment portfolio during the period you are taking income. The number of your annuity units is fixed, and does not change.

assumed interest rate (AIR): The rate of interest an annuity provider uses in determining the amount of each variable annuity income payment. Also known as the benchmark rate or the hurdle rate.

annuity purchase rate: The cost of an annuity based on insurance company tables, which take into account various factors such as your age and gender.

commutable contract: An annuity contract that allows you to terminate an annuitization agreement that is paying you income on a fixed period or fixed percentage basis.

contract value: The combined total of your principal and portfolio earnings in a variable annuity, up to and including the date on which you annuitize. Also known as accumulated value.

deferred annuity: An annuity contract that you purchase either with a single premium or with periodic payments to help save for retirement. With a deferred annuity, you can choose the point at which you convert the accumulated principal and earnings in your contract to a stream of income.

expense ratio: The amount, as a percentage of your total annuity account value, that you pay annually for operating, management, and insurance expenses.

fixed annuity: An annuity contract that guarantees you will earn a stated rate of interest during the accumulation phase of a deferred annuity, and that you will receive a fixed amount of income on a regular schedule when you annuitize.

guaranteed death benefit: The assurance that your beneficiaries will receive at least the amount you put into the annuity and typically your locked-in earnings if you die before beginning to take income. This guarantee is one of the insurance benefits that annuities provide.

immediate annuity: An annuity contract that you buy with a lump sum and begin to receive income from within a short period, always less than 13 months. An immediate annuity can be either fixed or variable.

income options: The various methods of receiving annuity income that an annuity contract offers. You may choose from among them the one that suits your situation best. Typically, there are six or more choices, many guaranteeing income for life.

investment portfolio: A collection of individual investments chosen by a professional manager to produce a clearly defined investment objective. Portfolios, which are structured the same way as open-end mutual funds, are offered in a variable annuity contract and are available to people who purchase the contract. They are also called subaccounts or investment accounts.

market value adjustment: This feature, which is included in some annuity contracts, imposes an adjustment, or fee, if you surrender your fixed annuity or the fixed account of your variable annuity. The adjustment offsets any losses the insurance company might incur in liquidating assets to pay the amount due to you.

nonqualified annuity: An annuity contract you buy individually rather than as part of an employer-sponsored qualified retirement plan. You pay the premium with after-tax dollars. With a deferred nonqualified annuity, your principal grows tax deferred.

premium: The amount you pay to buy an annuity or any other insurance product. With a single premium annuity you pay just once, but with other types you pay an initial premium and then make additional premium payments.

principal: The amount of money you use to purchase an annuity, bond, mutual fund, stock or other investment. The principal is the base on which your earnings accumulate.

proprietary portfolios: The investment portfolios offered within a variable annuity that are run by the insurance company's investment managers. The annuity may also offer portfolios run by managers working for another financial institution, such as a mutual fund.

qualified annuity: An annuity contract you buy with pretax dollars as part of an employer-sponsored qualified retirement plan.

rollover: An IRA or qualified retirement plan that you move from one trustee to another is known as a rollover. You can roll over any qualified plan, including a qualified annuity, into an IRA, preserving its tax-deferred status.

separate account: The account established by the insurance company to hold the money you contribute to your variable annuity. It is separate from the company's general account, where fixed annuity premiums are deposited. Money in the separate account is not available to the company's creditors.

single premium annuity: This type of annuity contract is purchased with a one-time payment. All immediate annuities and some deferred nonqualified annuities are in this category.

subaccount: The investment portfolios offered in variable annuity contracts are sometimes referred to as subaccounts. The terms refers to their position as accounts held within the separate account of the insurance company offering the variable annuity.

tiered interest crediting: A policy used by some companies who credit different interest rates to a fixed annuity's cash surrender value than they do to its annuitization value. This means the interest rate you earn is based on whether you surrender the annuity for cash or annuitize the contract for at least a minimum period and agree to the company's rules about how and when you can access your money. Typically, the rate is significantly higher if you choose the annuitization option. When comparing contracts, it's important to know if the rate you're being quoted applies to the cash surrender value or the annuitization value.

underlying investments: The stocks, bonds, cash equivalents or other investments purchased by a variable annuity portfolio or mutual fund with the money you and other people allocate to that portfolio or fund.

unit value: The dollar value of a single accumulation or annuity unit, which changes constantly to reflect the current combined total value of the underlying investments in your investment portfolios, minus expenses.

variable annuity: An annuity contract that allows you to allocate your premium among a number of investment portfolios. Your contract value, which can fluctuate in the short term, reflects the performance of the underlying investments held in those portfolios, minus the contract expenses.

INDEX

INDEX

Q

R

S

INDEX

Source: © Stocks, Bonds, Bills and Inflation 2001 Yearbook, Ibbotson Associates, Chicago (annually updates work by Roger G. Ibbotson and Rex A. Sinquefield). Used with permission. All rights reserved. Stocks are represented by the Standard & Poor's 500 Composite Index, an unmanaged index widely regarded as an indicator of domestic stock market performance. The S&P 500 does not take sales charge into consideration. Investors cannot purchase indices directly. Bonds are represented by long-term government bonds using a one-bond portfolio with a maturity near 20 years. Cash is represented by U.S. Treasury bills rolling over each month a one-bill portfolio containing, at the beginning of each month, the bill having the shortest maturity not less than one month. Inflation is based on the Consumer Price Index. Average annual returns include dividend or interest reinvestment. Past performance does not guarantee future results.

BOOKS FROM LIGHTBULB PRESS

Lightbulb Press books are available in bookstores everywhere. Visit us on the World Wide Web at www.lightbulbpress.com. Contact us at 212-485-8800 for information on quantity discounts.

THE WALL STREET JOURNAL GUIDE TO UNDERSTANDING MONEY & INVESTING
by Kenneth M. Morris and Virginia B. Morris

The ideal introduction to investing—and the perfect reference for the experienced investor. Over 1,000,000 copies sold.

Stocks ● Bonds ● Mutual Funds ● Indexes ● Risk/Return ● Tracking Performance ● Evaluating Companies ● Investing Online

THE WALL STREET JOURNAL GUIDE TO PLANNING YOUR FINANCIAL FUTURE
by Kenneth M. Morris and Virginia B. Morris

An all-inclusive guide to retiring in comfort, including the information you need to make smart long-term decisions.

Investment Strategies ● Salary Reduction Plans ● Social Security ● Insurance ● Pension Plans ● Long-term Care ● Estate Planning

THE WALL STREET JOURNAL GUIDE TO UNDERSTANDING PERSONAL FINANCE
by Kenneth M. Morris and Virginia B. Morris

The basics of personal finance—and the pitfalls to avoid along the way in everyday financial life.

Bank Accounts ● Credit Cards ● Mortgages ● Financial Planning ● College Education ● Investing ● Online Banking ● Taxes ● Planning for Retirement

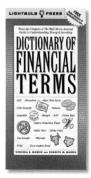

DICTIONARY OF FINANCIAL TERMS
by Virginia B. Morris and Kenneth M. Morris

The most important investing terms people hear and read every day—explained in language everyone can understand. Free online updates at www.lightbulbpress.com.

Hundreds of Definitions ● Financial Acronyms ● The Difference between Markets and Exchanges ● Reading a Stock Ticker ● Tracking the Markets

ESSENTIAL GUIDE TO YOUR 401(k) PLAN

by Virginia B. Morris and Kenneth M. Morris

Over 40 million Americans contribute to 401(k) plans. This guide takes the mystery out of retirement savings plans and explains how to create and manage an investment portfolio, roll over your account when you change jobs, and handle withdrawals when you retire.

Making Contributions • Employer Matching Plans • Tax Benefits • Choosing Investments • Allocating Assets • Transferring Funds • Vesting • Borrowing • Beneficiaries

A WOMAN'S GUIDE TO INVESTING

by Virginia B. Morris and Kenneth M. Morris
Introduction by Bridget A. Macaskill

The essential information—and inspiration—women of all ages need to manage their financial lives.

Setting Financial Goals • Making Smart Investment Decisions • Choosing a Financial Advisor • Investing with and without a Partner • Dealing with the Expected and Unexpected

A WOMAN'S GUIDE TO PERSONAL FINANCE

by Virginia B. Morris and Karen W. Lichtenberg

The guide every woman should read to learn how to plan her finances to meet her life's goals, secure a comfortable retirement, or manage a business.

Building a Financial Base • Planning for Different Stages in Your Life • Potential Hurdles • Protecting Your Resources • Planning for a Secure Retirement • Your Financial Legacy • Managing Your Business

GUIDE TO UNDERSTANDING ISLAMIC INVESTING

by Virginia B. Morris and Brian D. Ingram
Introduction by Shaykh Yusuf Talal DeLorenzo

This groundbreaking guide provides the information and guidance that Muslims need to make informed investment choices while conducting their financial lives in accordance with Islamic principles.

Diversifying your Portfolio • Evaluating Companies • Islamic Equity Mutual Funds • Zakah and Hajj • Halal and Haram

GUIDE TO CHOOSING, SERVING & ENJOYING WINE

by Allen R. Balik and Virginia B. Morris
Foreword by R. Michael Mondavi

A sparkling guide that uncorks the myths about choosing, serving, and enjoying wine and includes tips from famous winemakers and restaurateurs.

Ordering Wine in a Restaurant • Matching Wine with Food • Tasting and Judging Wines • Entertaining Guests at Home • Starting a Wine Collection